Corey~

    Always remember that <u>LOVE</u>

makes ♥ all the difference!

            Amber Cantona

Half Pint

"I am one of millions who raised their children on Dr. James Dobson's parenting principles. I am also one of the millions of Christians who would have been counted among Dobson's army of evangelical voices speaking to our nation's political powers about the decay of moral and family structure in the culture. While I long ago left the grip of manipulation, exaggerations, and hypocrisy sourced with Dobson and the Focus on the Family organization, Amber grew up in the midst of it. She gives her readers an intimate perspective of her Dobson-esque family with the imposed stress for imagined Christian perfection. Her memoir of the damage along with the struggle to survive and overcome the toxic grip of her family is worthy of reading."
—Kathy Baldock, founder and executive director of Canyonwalker Connections, author of *Walking the Bridgeless Canyon*

"Focus on the Family has had an immeasurable impact on the Christian family. This organization that has been embraced across denominational lines has long set the standard of what a Christian family ought to look like. Unfortunately, the ideologies of this organization—everything from how purity culture is taught to its rejection of LGBTQ identities—have caused untold damage to so many of its adherents.

In *Refocusing My Family*, Amber Cantorna is able to share honestly about her own struggles of growing up within the organization. Through these pages, she lifts the covers off of harmful practices to bring much needed nuance to the Christian faith. Amber is a remarkable testament of how God was able to break the spiritual and mental chains that had kept her from being her true self. I hope and pray this book is widely read."
—Danny Cortez, copastor of New Heart Community Church, Whittier, California

"Amber's book, *Refocusing My Family*, crystallizes the unique journey of LGBTQ people who have conservative, evangelical parents and families. Her intense fight for love and life itself is on every page of this important, life-giving book. A must-read!"
—Susan Cottrell, author of *"Mom, I'm Gay,"* founder and president of FreedHearts

"Amber writes a courageous deep dive into her experience in and out of the closet. Her memoir, *Refocusing My Family*, will help many young people struggling to live an authentic life. Her words touch the heart and offer hope."

—Gayani DeSilva, MD, author of *A Psychiatrist's Guide: Helping Parents Reach Their Depressed Tween*

"You will cry and you will cheer as Amber Cantorna shares her journey of overcoming tremendous difficulties in order to live her life authentically while still honoring her core values and beliefs. *Refocusing My Family* is the kind of story that has the power to change the world into a kinder, safer, more loving place for all of us to live."

—Liz Dyer, founder and owner of Serendipitydodah for Moms (a private Facebook group for moms of LGBTQ kids)

"Conservative, evangelical Christianity cannot come to terms with the stubborn fact that 3 to 5 percent of the human family is LGBTQ. They have cornered themselves into a place where accepting this fact is theologically impossible. Therefore, when one of their own children turns out to be a part of this sexual/gender minority, it creates an extraordinary crisis for families, churches, and, above all, for the LGBTQ person.

Amber Cantorna has survived this crisis. But it was a near thing. Her story is equally tragic and inspiring. It is tragic that her physical, emotional, and spiritual survival comes at the cost of her relationship with her Focus on the Family parents. But she has made the right choice. I applaud her courage, I pray for her flourishing, and I hope that within our lifetime, stories like hers will no longer have to be told."

—David Gushee, president of the Society of Christian Ethics, president-elect of the American Academy of Religion

"I have spent my professional life as a storyteller. I have had the great pleasure of meeting and working with so many people from across a broad spectrum of issues and points of view. Rarely have I been as struck by a personal story as I have by Amber's. Hers is a story of redemption in a world that requires people to live in confined boxes. In our current political and social climate, her story resonates, opens eyes, and proves that Christ's love is bigger than those who try to control it."

—Patrick Jager, CEO of CORE Innovation Group, award-winning television producer

"At once both intimate and deeply affecting, Amber Cantorna's moving memoir powerfully unpacks the shame and self-loathing so often felt by those caught in the crosshairs of conservative Christianity and sexual identity. Her ultimate redemption comes when she is finally able to step beyond the confines of her Focus on the Family upbringing to find unconditional love among her new chosen family. A must read!"

—Daniel Karslake, director/producer of *For the Bible Tells Me So* and *For They Know Not What They Do*

"The all-too-common practice of rejecting LGBTQ children from their Christian families is a religious tragedy Amber Cantorna has experienced firsthand. Yet, exiled from her family home, Amber clung to the assurance of things hoped for. Thank you, Amber, for sharing what it is like to walk the gay Christian crucible of faith toward dignity, healing, and most miraculous of all—love."

—Jennifer Knapp, Dove Award winning artist, singer/songwriter/author, founder of Inside Out Faith Foundation

"In our family, we focus on two core things: being brave and being kind. After reading *Refocusing My Family*, it is clear to me that Amber must be the sister I never had. The sheer bravery she displays—not just in *telling* this story, but first in *living* it out—is astounding. It is matched only by the kindness she shows—both to herself and to the family that rejected her. May Amber's story do for you what it did for me: teach me that it will only be through the stories of the marginalized that the church has hope for finding the healing it so desperately needs."

—Colby Martin, author of *UnClobber: Rethinking Our Misuse of the Bible on Homosexuality*

"Literally millions of us trusted James Dobson and Focus on the Family to guide us in raising the ideal Christian family. Amber Cantorna's book, *Refocusing My Family*, pulls back the curtain and reveals the real-life realities behind Focus's books, purity rings, and radio shows. I hope that today's young parents who are part of the evangelical community will allow Amber's story to guide them into a better way of parenting, so they can discover a more authentic way of being Christians—and human beings, too."

—Brian D. McLaren, author of *The Great Spiritual Migration*

"In *Refocusing My Family*, Amber Cantorna gives us the privilege of stepping into her remarkable story; one she tells with clarity, vulnerability, and great courage. It is a raw and unflinching walk through the treacherous minefield of being both gay and Christian in a world that tells you these things are incompatible. It is at times heartbreaking and other times overflowing with hope, as all our stories are—which is the point. In *Refocusing My Family*, Amber reminds us that our desire to be known and loved is universal. Step into her story and you will surely find yours as well."

—John Pavlovitz, author of *A Bigger Table: Building Messy, Authentic, and Hopeful Spiritual Community*

"*Refocusing My Family* is as much a harrowing tale of one woman's struggle to swim up to the surface as it is an indictment of the deadening consequences of bad religion that holds people under in the name of all things holy."

—Mark Tidd, founder and copastor of Highlands Church, Denver, Colorado

"Amber Cantorna's story of growing up gay and Christian will resonate with anyone who has struggled with feeling different or not fitting the mold. Her bravery and perseverance will inspire other LGBTQ people, and her love for her faith will change many hearts and minds in the church. This is an important book for all Christians to read and share, and I am very grateful to Amber for writing it."

—Matthew Vines, executive director of The Reformation Project, author of *God and the Gay Christian*

"No amount of theological posturing has the power of a story well told, and Amber Cantorna's *Refocusing My Family* is a beautiful narrative of the journey from torment and shame to authenticity and hope. Wherever you find yourself in the LGBTQ debate, this book will get you thinking about what really matters."

—Paula Stone Williams, national transgender advocate and former megachurch preaching pastor

REFOCUSING
MY FAMILY

REFOCUSING MY FAMILY

COMING OUT, BEING CAST OUT, AND DISCOVERING THE TRUE LOVE OF GOD

AMBER CANTORNA

FORTRESS PRESS
MINNEAPOLIS

REFOCUSING MY FAMILY
Coming Out, Being Cast Out, and Discovering the True Love of God

Cover image: Brooke Marcellino of Josie Pix
Cover design: Brad Norr
Book design: PerfecType, Nashville, TN
Author photo: Nick Velharticky

ISBN: 978-1-5064-1879-7
eBook ISBN: 978-1-5064-1880-3

The paper used in this publication meets the minimum requirements of American National Standard for Information Sciences — Permanence of Paper for Printed Library Materials, ANSI Z329.48-1984.

Manufactured in the U.S.A.

To every LGBTQ person who feels that their love or gender identity somehow disqualifies them from the love of God, and to every parent who fears for their child: May God redeem beauty from ashes and heal all the heartache in you.

CONTENTS

FOREWORD

My husband Rob and I raised our kids on "Adventures in Odyssey," the weekly radio show from Focus on the Family. We measured our road trips by them: "Just five more Odysseys until we get there, kids!" From Eugene's madcap misadventures in time machines, to Connie's parents' divorce, we took comfort in Whit's constant love, wisdom, and compassion. One summer we took our kids to visit the real Whit's End at the Focus on the Family headquarters in Colorado Springs. We took pictures of the kids with a life-sized cutout of Whit, and we sat at the soda fountain with a Wod-Fam-Choc-Sod (World Famous Chocolate Soda). The stories reinforced the conservative, Christian values we were faithfully instilling in our five kids throughout our years of home-schooling and church community, and we raised five beautiful children into adulthood.

Then, when our daughter Annie was twenty, she called and told me she was attracted to girls. She'd felt this way for a long time, she'd tried to deny it, but she couldn't make it go away. I did not see it coming, and I was stunned. This was our beloved Annie-girl—how did we not see this?

Surprisingly (given our church involvement), I was not horrified, as so many evangelical parents are. I'd had gay and

Susan Cottrell's kids at Focus on the Family's 'Whit's End', 2000

lesbian friends over the years, and they were lovely. My kids had gay friends from their theater involvement.

My big concern was for Annie. *What will become of her, will she be safe, what does this mean about her faith—and ours?* And right in that moment, another thought came to mind: *We will never be the same in the church again.* No one had outlined the church's position on homosexuality, but I instinctively knew that the church was no longer a safe place for us. It was not a haven, definitely not a "sanctuary," and that realization was earth-shattering.

What emerged was the clear distinction between the gospel of Jesus and *the non-affirming church.*

Jesus showed us that love always wins, love is the beginning and end of the gospel message, and love is every point in between. Love *is* God's way. Our home-school co-op and youth group involvement had shown us that when we put rules above relationship, we hurt people. We'd seen it time and again—children driven to despair by parents who hold them to their own standard for that child, instead of embracing the child God gave them, exactly as they are. We saw that *un*-love is deadly.

But none of that came to mind that day on the phone with Annie. What came to mind is that I love my daughter fiercely and nothing would come between us. Jesus loves her unconditionally, to the ends of the earth. Period. Who am I to put conditions on my love for my child? Rob and I never wavered in that truth, not for a moment. We never considered the possibility that we would sever relationship with *any* of our kids, ever. How could we? *Why* would we?

Imagine my shock, then, when Annie asked me if I was sure we would never kick her out of our lives. "Of course not," I answered.

"Never?" she persisted. "You or Dad? Are you sure?"

I stared at her. "No, Annie, never—but *why do you keep asking?"*

"Because so many of my friends have been disowned by their families," she said.

I was stunned.

That's when it hit me: *the church is in real trouble.* It does not know the difference between the love of Christ and punishment for the noncompliant. I already knew that the conservative, evangelical church extracts a high price for noncompliance. I'd seen it in parents who were raising stellar kids, but who were never quite satisfied—they constantly wanted their kids to stand up straighter or tuck in their shirt. But I did not know that parents were throwing out their gay children.

My husband and I worked through the theology, for our own peace of mind, and we were shocked that the verses that are said to condemn homosexuality aren't even talking about homosexuality as we know it. Those verses relate more to the priest sex scandal and sex trafficking than to adult relationships of mutual consent. The more we prayed, the more we knew that love is the way. I knew I needed to help the LGBTQI community that was being rejected, and I needed to help their families know there is a better way.

That's when I founded FreedHearts, our nonprofit ministry to parents, their LGBTQI children, and the faith community. I wrote *"Mom, I'm Gay"—Loving Your LGBTQ Child and Strengthening Your Faith*, and *True Colors: Celebrating the Truth and Beauty of the Real You*, a workbook to help LGBTQI heal from family, religious, and community wounds. All the while, organizations such as Focus on the Family—on whom families have depended for years for Christian insight—teach toxic messages of rejection instead of embrace, judgment instead of love, fracture instead of unity.

When Amber Cantorna introduced herself to me at a Gay Christian Network conference, I was delighted to meet such a beautiful, gentle, loving woman, and her equally lovely wife, Clara. When she told me her parents had rejected her, I was grieved, but not shocked. What did shock me was that Amber's father worked at Focus on the Family, and Amber had grown up on "Adventures in Odyssey." I'd hoped that those closest to Focus would live out the Christian and family values they claimed. But no. How ironic that a ministry that claims to *focus on the family* instead focuses on reputation, rules, and being right. When Amber told me she was writing her story, I was glad, because it's a story that needs to be told. The non-affirming church needs to know that its actions are hurting innocent children, that they are cutting off the ones they were told to care for. Frightened and hurting parents need to understand that throwing out their children is never God's answer.

Her story is at once compelling, heartbreaking, and full of hope. This journey has cost her, but she has also been freed. Her love and beauty and heart shine through, and her life has been restored.

Mr. Whittaker said in an Odyssey episode, "God puts those passions in our heart for a reason." God put passions in Amber's heart for a reason, too. I imagine if Whit could read her story, he might shake his head and say, "Jesus wants us to focus on *love*, not being right—on coming together, not breaking apart." I also imagine he'd like that the story has a happy ending.

Amber's story of life, love, and restoration is one adventure you don't want to miss.

Susan Cottrell
Founder and President, FreedHearts

PROLOGUE

I hadn't journaled for almost four years. At the age of twenty-seven, I had a secret. A secret so powerful, it silenced not only my voice, but my pen as well. A secret I was afraid to admit, even to myself. Overwhelmed with shame and full of guilt, I was powerless to put it on paper. I was terrified that by writing it down, it would become too real for my soul to bear. I wasn't ready to be that real.

For four years, I struggled with my sexuality. It was a suffocating journey that deprived me of words most of the time. Admitting a romantic attraction toward people of the same gender was unthinkable for any Christian, but even more so for a Christian with *my* background: my father is an executive at Focus on the Family. He's worked there almost all my life. With that company name as the trademark of our family, I didn't think I could ever let my secret out. Yet it followed me daily, begging for my attention. So I took my secret to the only place that I knew it would be safe: counseling. Granting myself the permission I desperately needed to process my feelings and fears that lurked in the darkness, I slowly came to grips with the reality that I am gay.

That realization caused me to feel disjointed, like I didn't fit in anywhere. It was as if half of me belonged in one world, and half of me in another. Both worlds coexisted in my heart yet refused to cohabitate in real life. I stood at a crossroads. I refused to lie or be a hypocrite, but I knew that if my secret were found out in church, I would no longer be allowed to serve in ministry. Torn and conflicted, I engaged in a mental war day and night—a war I couldn't escape, because it raged inside of me. This internal war was so brutal, it produced external scars; self-injury was the only way I knew to survive. Eventually, I began to wonder if the struggle was worth it. I wondered if it would be better to be dead.

In a final attempt to free my soul, I searched the internet to see if churches that were both biblically sound *and* accepting of the LGBTQ community even existed. It was the only option I could think of that might save me. Looking outside my hometown of Colorado Springs, I found a nondenominational church in Denver. Upon reading their ethos, I was immediately inspired by their transparency and intrigued by their model for living. Reaching out to the pastor, I quickly received a heartfelt invitation to visit.

January 8, 2012, was the day I attended Highlands Church for the very first time. I found and met people like me that day, and for the first time in four years, I felt a little less isolated, and a little more hopeful. It seemed my journey might not have to end after all.

Up to that point, I'd been afraid to write the words, as if doing so gave them permission, validity, and life. But the day I visited Highlands Church was a turning point for me, like crossing a threshold into a new and totally different reality. That day, I finally penned the words that I'd hidden inside for so long, "I am gay."

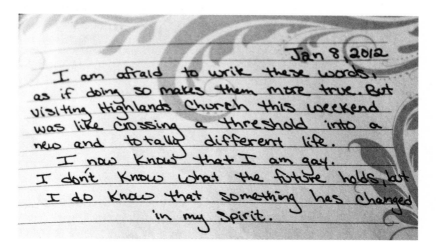

Jan 8, 2012

I am afraid to write these words, as if doing so makes them more true. But visiting Highlands Church this weekend was like crossing a threshold into a new and totally different life.

I now know that I am gay. I don't know what the future holds, but I do know that something has changed in my spirit.

I passed the point of no return. I could feel it. Something changed in my spirit. The story that unfolded in the months and years to follow is the story you'll read in this book. Whether you're a parent, a pastor, a friend, or an LGBTQ person searching for answers on your own journey through faith and sexuality, my desire is that through my story, you'll not only find your story, but you'll also find the courage and the hope you need to live it out.

The point in writing this book is not to berate Focus on the Family, nor is it meant to denigrate my parents. Rather, my goal is to give a voice to LGBTQ people who are living this same story in different families and churches all around the world. I pray that my story will shine light on the damage that beliefs like those of Focus on the Family inflict on real people.

And I hope that through my story, we can learn to love a little more like Jesus did—and does—love us.

As you read about the journey I took to refocus my family, may you find light, courage, and strength to continue on your own path as well.

*Trigger Warning:** Self-injury is discussed in detail in short segments of chapters 5, 6, and 9. If this could be potentially triggering for you, please keep yourself safe and skip the paragraphs marked with an *.

Note: All names in this book have been used with permission or changed for the sake of privacy.

1

MY ADVENTURE
IN ODYSSEY

"Okay, Amber, we're ready for you. Let's head on back to the recording studio and get you set up."

I hopped off the stool where I waited for my cue and followed the engineer into the soundproof recording booth.

"Have a seat right here, honey. This microphone is for you," he explained, walking over with me to help me get situated. I placed my script on the music stand in front of me and plopped myself down in the chair.

"Here are your headphones. Just put them on your ears like this," he continued, as he adjusted the wide black strap across the top of my head and placed an earphone over each ear. They felt like a pair of winter earmuffs, only much heavier. My head bobbed at the weight of them, and the suction they created around my ears muted all sound, causing the world to go silent.

Then a loud, clear voice from within the earphones broke the dead air. The sound came from a man on the other side of the glass where the engineers sat in front of their mixing boards, ready to record.

"Okay, Amber, let's test the microphone. Do you have your script?"

"Yes, but I already know my lines." I smiled with pride.

"Alright, then here we go!"

• • • • •

I was a home-schooled third-grader. When most kids visit their dad at work, they go to an office, or a storefront. I, on the other hand, was in a recording studio at the Focus on the Family headquarters in Colorado Springs where my dad worked as an executive. The script on the music stand in front of me was to another episode of the popular kids' radio drama, "Adventures

Will Ryan (Eugene Meltsner) and me

in Odyssey." Venturing into the world of Whit's End with characters like Mr. John Avery Whittaker, Connie Kendall, and Eugene Meltsner, a "world of discovery, imagination, and excitement" awaited all who listened.

I listened multiple times to every episode ever made. I knew them all by name, which cassette or CD package to find them on, and the story line of each. The episodes of "Adventures in Odyssey" helped me fall asleep at night, gauged the time remaining on a road trip, and made cleaning my room a little easier. The excitement of playing one of the characters was only matched by seeing the details of how the episodes were created. I loved watching the actors record, listening as the voice parts were mixed with music to create smooth transitions between scenes, and seeing how foley (the sound-effects) made the whole story come to life. But the "world of discovery, imagination, and excitement" didn't just live within the fantasy of Whit's End; it also lived within my everyday life—especially my home life. From the time I was very young, I was taught the utmost importance of one thing: family.

· · · · ·

"Cherry Coke, Daddy! Cherry Coke!" I begged as a toddler inside the nursery of our home in Kalispell, Montana. I pulled at my dad's pant leg and looked up at him until he relented. Smiling down, he picked me up, threw me up in the air, and caught me. I'd giggle and say, "Again, Daddy! Again!"

For as far back as I can remember, I was the apple of my father's eye. From butterfly kisses to Saturday-morning cuddles to Cherry Cokes, we shared a special bond that can only be created between a dad and his little girl. He delighted in me as his only daughter, and with a twinkle in his eye, often made a point to tell me, "I'm so proud of you, Am."

My parents worked hard to incorporate values that James Dobson and Focus on the Family deemed important, which really came down to two foundational commands: love God with all your heart, and foster a godly family. Family was the ultimate gift and should reflect Christ in all aspects. Principles like the sanctity of marriage, the belief that every life is valuable, and the fact that children should be raised with morals grounded in biblical principles all pointed back to loving God. That's how you focused on your family.

My parents modeled many of these things well. With the belief that family is more important than work, they made it a priority to be present in the lives of me and my younger brother, Daniel, as we grew up. Thankfully, working at Focus allowed my father more leeway than many when it came to being an active parent. Always tucking me into bed at night and praying with me for sweet dreams and protection, my dad often sang:

> *You're the spirit of Christmas, my star on the tree*
> *You're the Easter bunny, to Mommy and me*
> *You're sugar and spice, you're everything nice*
> *And you're Daddy's little girl*[1]

I never doubted that I was loved.

But leaving our safe home near relatives in Montana to accept a job at Focus and discover life in the outskirts of Los Angeles was a risk for us. Years later my dad told me that when we arrived in California, he was so frightened by what he saw

---

1. The Mills Brothers, "Daddy's Little Girl," 1950.

that he wanted turn around and head straight back to Montana. This was *not* where he wanted to raise his family. But trusting God's providence, he stayed, and now thirty years later my dad is still employed as an executive at Focus.

However, he was grateful in 1991 when Focus relocated to beautiful Colorado Springs. Anxious to get away from the inner-city feel and into a smaller town, my parents purchased a home in a quiet neighborhood on the north end of the city, only a short drive from the new Focus headquarters. The epicenter for many major Christian ministries, Colorado Springs quickly felt like home, and we put down new roots.

Early on, my mom made home-schooling my brother and me her passion. Not wanting us to attend the below-average public school in our neighborhood, and not being able to afford private school, it seemed like the best fit for raising "godly" children. Home-schooling was popular among Christians in Colorado Springs, so we continued to flourish in that environment. Networking and doing co-ops with other home-school families, my mom picked out curriculum for each subject and prepared a detailed schedule to keep us on task each day. Our mornings always started with individual quiet time with God, followed by getting dressed and being ready for family breakfast and devotions at 7am.

Our days were highly structured, but after lunch Danny and I could be found lying on our beds, listening to "Adventures in Odyssey." Like a Christian Disneyland for the ears, the twenty-five-minute radio programs kept us occupied and engaged, while teaching us Christian morals and values like honesty, integrity, and service to others. Although it was a nice break in our day, my mom knew that allowing time for us to listen to an episode

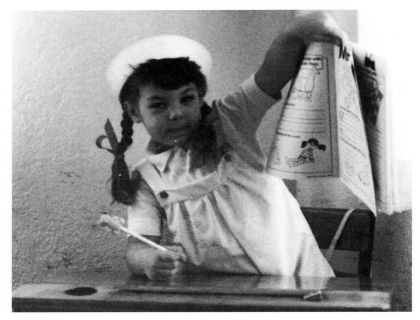

My first day of school

wasn't just entertainment; it was another avenue for us to learn the morals she and my dad were trying hard to instill in us. They used the episodes as a springboard to teach us an overarching family value. For instance, in the episode "Fences," when Connie Kendall is upset that her father cancels his trip to Odyssey, the theme emphasized throughout the story is dealing with disappointment and the importance of communication. In "Treasures of the Heart" when the Barclay family holds a yard sale to clean up their cluttered attic, but finds keepsakes that hold varying degrees of value for them, the lesson is setting proper priorities on material things. Some episodes also highlight a certain historical character or event, like the three-part series "The Underground Railroad" or "Pilgrim's Progress Revisited."

Each episode we listened to taught values like manners, respect, and the importance of cultivating your own relationship with God—values my parents hoped we would pick up on and incorporate into our own lives as we grew up.

When "Adventures in Odyssey" celebrated its tenth year, Focus on the Family headquarters hosted a special event where an episode of the show was recorded in front of a live audience. Key actors were flown in from Los Angeles and my brother and I both played a part. Families from all over were encouraged to attend, which meant lines were long, the house was packed, and people buzzed with excitement.

Paul Herlinger (Mr. Whittaker) and me

*Recording the 'Adventures in Odyssey' live episode
for its tenth year anniversary celebration*

When everyone was in place and ready to begin, the theme song played and the lights went down.

"Hi, this is Chris. Welcome to Adventures in Odyssey!" The famous first words of the show came through loud and clear.

Each of us bantered through our lines together and music played to transition us from scene to scene. A couple of guys on the side of the stage did live foley throughout the show so you could see how the sound effects were actually created. The crowd was fully engaged.

Following the recording, we all sat behind a long table as people lined up to collect autographs. They bought T-shirts, CD packages, and the newly released book, "The Complete Guide to Adventures in Odyssey," and worked their way down the line so that each of the actors could sign their mementos from the day.

"Will you sign this for me?" a cute little girl in pigtails asked, with her Odyssey T-shirt in one hand and her doll in the other.

"Of course," I said with a smile. "What's your doll's name?" I asked as I personalized her T-shirt for her. I was an early teenager at the time, but remembered my doll-playing days well.

As a little girl, I loved dressing up my dolls and playing house. I dreamed about my future with a husband and family of my own to raise on the same Focus foundation I was reared on. I did not dream that I would be married to a woman and that my dad's position at Focus would divide me from my family rather than keep us focused on it—but that's what happened. I got married to my wife Clara in 2014 without any family present

Signing autographs at the 'Adventures in Odyssey' tenth year anniversary event held at Focus on the Family

to support me and with my relationship with my parents hanging by a thread.

When Clara was five years old, she already knew she was attracted to girls—but not me. When I was five, I innocently played with my Cabbage Patch doll named Holly Dolly and imagined a future family very similar to the one I was being raised in. It included a good husband, a cultivated family environment, kids with a home-schooled upbringing, and loads of holiday traditions.

My parents worked hard to model a healthy relationship and were conscientious about not arguing in front of us kids. I imagined a marriage that looked very similar to theirs. Looking back, I'm very grateful that I didn't grow up in a house of dissension. I'm grateful not to have memories of my parents yelling at one another or at us. I'm sure that is something they worked hard for.

But this also created an aura of perfection and didn't provide the opportunity for me to learn that conflict is normal. Since their disagreements always took place behind closed doors, I never got to see my parents model healthy disagreement and resolution. As a result, I grew up believing that a normal life meant a happy life without conflict.

As I grew, I noticed even more that strong emotions—especially negative emotions—weren't welcome. We were taught to be happy, blessed, and respectful. There was little tolerance for laziness (the early bird gets the worm), messiness (cleanliness is next to godliness), or grumpiness (God never gives you more than you can handle). We were taught that everything happens for a reason and that having enough faith and praying more were the answer to all of life's problems.

In time, these limits on expression stunted my emotional growth. Without freedom to experiment with or vocalize other emotions like sadness, disappointment, or anger, I internalized those feelings. My parents' subtle disapproval of my emotions squelched my chance for healthy development.

. . . . .

Once a year, our church hosted a father-daughter dance. At the age of nine, I'd been anxiously waiting for this night for weeks. I was excited to dress up and have a night out with my dad all to myself. But peering out the window, the once-thin blanket of white had now tripled in depth and the storm showed no signs of slowing down. I got anxious, fear threatening to deflate my bubbly spirit.

Then the phone rang. I could hear my mom talking in the kitchen, but couldn't make out what she was saying. Still, I knew. Soon, she knocked on my bedroom door.

"Come in," I mumbled sadly. Mom opened the door to tell me the news she knew I didn't want to hear: the dance had been canceled due to inclement weather. I blinked back tears.

"Sometimes it's just better to not get your hopes up about things at all, Amber," she said. "That way you're not disappointed when they don't work out."

I know she meant well, grasping at whatever she could to make me feel better. But telling me not to get my hopes up or express disappointment caused me to withdraw, and left me feeling depressed rather than encouraged. Moments like those communicated to me that emotions other than happiness and joy are best kept inside, and from early childhood, I began compartmentalizing what I felt.

Excitement, though, was usually an acceptable emotion—especially around the holidays. My mom had a gift for making the holidays meaningful, special, and full of symbolism. With fall as her favorite time of year, her love for cool, crisp weather and vibrant aspens across the Rocky Mountains sparked the beginning of our Great Pumpkin Dinner tradition.

We went trick-or-treating in our younger years, but as we got older trick-or-treating was replaced with the Great Pumpkin Dinner. Gathering together in our home with friends, we started the festivities with the annual pumpkin-carving contest. Spreading old newspaper across the picnic table in the backyard, we each chose a pattern and took careful time and pride in crafting our designs. Once the carving was complete and candles glowed within them, we lined the pumpkins up for the ultimate display.

When the winner was announced and the applause subsided, we gathered around the table for a big fall potluck. Joining hands and offering a prayer, we then enjoyed a feast of apple cider beef stew (often cooked inside an actual pumpkin), pumpkin bread, orange soda, and anything else pumpkin-themed we could come up with. Later in the evening, we watched *It's the Great Pumpkin, Charlie Brown*. Sitting around the fireplace with caramel apples and hot apple cider in hand, we watched in anticipation as Linus sat in the field awaiting the Great Pumpkin's appearance. It never got old. In fact, it created such wonderful memories for me that it's a tradition my wife and I continue to hold to this day, each year hosting a new group of friends in our home to experience the Great Pumpkin extravaganza. I still always look forward to it. But fall is a bittersweet time for me. I think of my mom every year as I set the table for this event. I

The Great Pumpkin Dinner my wife and I hosted in 2015

wish she could see it. It's a tradition I enjoy upholding, but that joy is always accompanied by lingering sadness in my heart.

Christmas was always my favorite holiday of the year. My dad disguised himself as Santa Claus and came to visit us in his red suit each Christmas Eve. Pushing nostalgia as long as I could, I begged him to continue the tradition until I was twenty-two. As a kid, I never figured out why Santa always came at the exact time that my dad ran to the store to get 7 Up for the punch. But as we grew, we loved sitting on his lap for an annual photo and counted on the matching pajamas he brought in his sack for me and Mom, and likewise for Daniel and Dad. We went to bed each Christmas Eve snuggled up in new flannel warmth, smiling at the fact that Santa had come for yet another year. Trying hard to create a family bond and also fond family memories that we would look back on for years to come, Mom would often tell me, "Amber, friends will come and go, but your family will always be there for you."

I believed what she said. Trusting it, I shaped my view of the world around the concept that Cherry Coke and Santa Claus moments would always be there, and believed that focusing on my family should take priority above all else. I had no idea that in the future, my family would teach me something very different.

2

GROWING UP A
GREEN GABLE GIRL

Although my dad is the one who worked at Focus on the Family, my mom is the one who implemented those family values at home. Thankfully, my dad's job allowed him to be very present in our lives. Unless he was traveling, he never missed a performance or recital. But while my dad worked and traveled for his job, my mom stayed home to raise my brother and me. She loved being a wife, a mother, and a homemaker, and she was good at it. She focused a lot of time and energy not only in home-schooling us, but also in modeling a Christian lifestyle. I remember waking up in the morning and seeing both my parents reading their Bibles and praying. I remember them fasting and teaching us to do the same, not necessarily with food, but with things like TV or sweets. We always had meals together at the table, and breakfast time included family devotions and Scripture memorization. On top of it all, my mom kept a clean, cozy, and welcoming home that always felt peaceful and inviting. My parents did a lot of things very well.

The fact that I'm still carrying on the Great Pumpkin Dinner in my own home with my own family twenty years after she started the tradition is testament to that. I know that every time I get a compliment about how beautifully my home is decorated or what a lovely table I set for my guests, I owe it all to her. As a kid, I loved all the traditions we had around the holidays and looked forward to them more than anyone else in the family. But as an adult, I now realize the amount of time she invested in creating that family environment in our home, and I cherish those traditions even more.

My mom also started a club for me and other young girls. She teamed up with her best friend, Shaina, hoping that the club would not only help me make some friends as a home-schooled girl in a new town, but also provide an opportunity for me to do the things that young girls love. As a group of about eight girls, we had tea parties and sleepovers; we shared girlie secrets and played with dolls. Comprised mostly of home-schoolers, we got together on a monthly basis. Reading the young adult version of a fun classic like *Little Women*, my mom and Shaina followed up the discussion with specific craft projects that paired with the theme of the story. Of course, the ultimate classic in my household growing up was *Anne of Green Gables*. Anne was the epitome of a hopeless romantic, and her dramatic way of waltzing through life drew each of us in time and time again. Therefore, in honor of Anne, we named our club the Green Gable Girls (GGG).

The GGG club played a significant role in my childhood. Many of my fondest recollections are linked directly to a GGG play we put on, a Christmas tea we had, or a mother-daughter event we orchestrated. My childhood was filled

Wearing my new dress for one of our first Green Gable Girls events

with GGG moments that I still look back on with fondness and nostalgia.

· · · · ·

On my sweet sixteenth birthday, my GGG friends were invited over for high tea. Although often stuck hanging out with all us girls, my brother was a young gentleman and dressed up in a suit to escort each of the ladies in upon arrival. Both he and my dad were great sports and served in the role of our butlers for the evening, waiting on us hand and foot as we enjoyed our tea and scones with clotted cream. Then it was story time—only this story was not a memory of the past, but a foretelling of the future. My dad started the story by summarizing the first sixteen years of my life and then thrust my future into the hands of my all-too-willing friends. I sat, a bit embarrassed as they each in turn imagined a piece of my future, continuing the story from where the last person left off.

Collaborating in my fate together, a few things were clear:

- My husband would be dashingly handsome.
- I would go on a music tour across Europe.
- I would serve in music ministry with my husband for many years.
- We would have many babies together.

This was my future through the eyes of my dear friends. Kind, generous, and always good for a laugh, they were definitely, as Anne would say, my "kindred spirits." Whatever brought us together, we always enjoyed each other's company. Mom and Shaina both hoped their hard work would foster bonds of friendship to last a lifetime.

High tea with the GGGs

*Hannah and I grew up in GGGs together. Years later,
she stood as a bridesmaid in my wedding.*

Although I'm sure the circumstances now look very different from what my mom had in mind at the time, I'm still in touch with five out of those eight girls today. In fact, two of them have come back into my life as some of my best friends and strongest allies. One of them even stood as a bridesmaid in my wedding—she was there to support me, even when my own mother was not. My mom's mission of creating lifelong friends for me succeeded.

Both Mom and Shaina worked endlessly to make our times together not only fun, but meaningful and steeped in tradition and symbolism. They also made sure God was at the center of it all and taught us not only how to be young women of God, but also how to develop the traits that Proverbs 31 says make a godly wife and mother. Among those traits were working hard with your hands, speaking wisdom and faithful instruction to others, watching over the affairs of the household, not being idle, and getting up in the dark of night to provide food for your family—these characteristics set you apart and made you a wife of noble character with a worth far above rubies. Then, your children would call you blessed and your husband would praise you.[2] Etiquette and lady-like manners were important, but they were still secondary to things like humility, personal quiet time with God, and home-making skills. "Charm is deceitful and beauty is passing, but a woman who fears the Lord, she shall be praised." My mom and Shaina quoted this verse from Proverbs 31:30 to us often. They did their best to emulate what they hoped we would someday become.

But entering my mid-teens, I started feeling pressure to emulate those traits. With my mom as the leader, a certain expectation developed when it came to my own behavior. These girls looked up to my mother, and therefore looked up to me. Often their confidant, I was the one they would go to for support and advice. I even remember one of the girls once saying to me,

"With your dad's position at Focus and your mom leading this GGG group, your family must just be so perfect!"

No, my family was not perfect. It may have appeared that way from the outside, but the pressure I was feeling as a teenager from a dad with a well-known position at Focus and a mom who led the group that all my friends were a part of, began to weigh on me. My mom expected me to lead these girls by example. It was understood that I would always be kind and gracious and show up with a smile. Being a *blessing* to these girls was an assumed responsibility. I didn't even really understand what that meant. I just knew I was supposed to have a good attitude and be a positive role model for them. In time I learned that it

---

2. Proverbs 31:10–31 (NIV).

also meant I could no longer let my hair down and be one of the girls.

But "being a blessing" was a standard expectation for every area of life in our household. Whether performing somewhere, going to visit relatives, or hosting company in our home, it was essential to put other people's needs above our own. Before we'd arrive somewhere, my mom always made a point to tell us, "You need to go with the mindset that you're going to be a blessing to them." What that really meant was to be on our best behavior, but the term *blessing* gave it the Christian trademark.

Blessing others was especially important when it came to our musical gifts. Like Christianity, music was a part of my life from the time I was born. My mom came from a musical family that traveled and sang as a group in her teen years, so she instilled that same passion in both my brother and me from infancy. Singing my first solo in church just before I turned two sparked the beginning of a lifetime of musical performances. From that moment on, there was rarely a time I wasn't involved in a children's choir or performing in some capacity. My mom thrived on helping me with my latest recitation or vocal piece and I thrived on performing it. Music was an outlet that challenged me and also drew me closer to God. I found comfort in the way the lyrics and piano keys connected me to a form of expression. Since emotions were something I struggled to express honestly, pouring that honesty into my music lent me strength. I didn't have to find words to describe how I was feeling. Instead, I could show it in the sound my fingers created. To this day, the financial sacrifices my parents made to foster my musical gifts are still among the things I am most grateful for.

Winning a county-wide talent show at age three for
my recitation of "The Moon Came Too"

After hosting my first piano recital at the age of seven and seeing my talent quickly take off, my parents took me to a piano audition with a woman who had obtained her degree from the London Conservatory of Music. A sage woman, she prided herself on being strict but fair, and I met my match in her as she constantly gave me the challenge I sought. Competing in regional and district competitions frequently, I often came home with a blue ribbon or trophy to go with my big smile and sense of accomplishment.

My mom also devoted a lot of time to teaching Danny and me to sing. By the time I was nine, between vocal arrangements in three-part harmonies (Mom, my brother, and me), piano songs, and Scripture recitations, we had quite the repertoire and were putting on entire concerts by ourselves. Mom scheduled us to perform at nearby retirement homes, at private Christian schools, and at local churches. She was creative, and she had a knack for organizing these events. Dad was not musical, but he was supportive and willingly played the role of our sound engineer. He never failed to tell us how well we did or how proud he was of us.

I always loved performing and I'm grateful that my mom instilled that passion in me from such a young age. My early childhood experience with music later opened up opportunities for me to travel with both national and international musical groups in my teen years. Music shaped me. I thrived

Winning one of my first piano competitions

Performing my first solo piano recital, age seven

Performing for a Christian school

on it and always looked forward to the next musical challenge or opportunity. While Green Gable Girls was where I went to have fun and be a girl, music is where I went to be inspired and challenged.

Both became ways I connected with my mom, and I gleaned from her not only as a leader, but also as a role model. Regardless of what she put her hands to do, blessing others was always front and center to her. So for me, growing up in a Focus, home-schooled environment, "being a blessing" just became part of common, everyday life.

Something I've learned in hindsight though is that blessing others often came with a hidden caveat. There was an unspoken mentality among Christians in general that divided the world into two groups. There was *us* (those who were Christian, those who were home-schooled, those who followed the teachings of Focus and of God—in other words, those who were *right*) and then there was *them* (the secular world—meaning anyone who was not a Christian and therefore not like us). Catholics weren't really Christians. Mormons definitely weren't Christians. Secular teenagers were rebellious. Those who went to public school were exposed to too much. Homosexuals were sexually loose and responsible for corrupting our society. And those who didn't trust God for their future had a hard road ahead.

"You should be grateful that you have the family you have, Amber. Most kids aren't as fortunate as you," my mom frequently told me. And in many ways she was right. I was very fortunate. But the problem with this mentality is that it created a hierarchy. Rather than seeing everyone as equal, it put us above everybody else. It made us better than them, more knowledgeable than them, more spiritual than them. In turn, "being a blessing" to others became a form of charity—something we did to help those less fortunate than us. And in helping them, the goal was always to make them more like us. Our gifts of blessing rarely came without strings attached. The unspoken expectation was that whatever we were doing to help them would hopefully bring them one step closer to becoming good, Jesus-loving Christians who did what the Bible commanded.

Nowadays, more than ever in my life, I choose to surround myself with people who are different from me—especially people with different religious beliefs. Some of my best friends today are Mormons, Catholics, atheists, and agnostics. Spending time with them adds much richness to my life. They bring me closer, not further away, from the person of Jesus. They broaden my thinking and challenge my worldview. I agree that our lives should bless and bring light and life to others, but to be like Christ, it must come without conditions. In order for me to learn that lesson though, I had to get off the ladder of hierarchy. And that was going to take some time on the path of humility.

3

MY THIRTEEN-YEAR-OLD
VOW TO PURITY

I grew up in the heart of the purity culture. True Love Waits campaigns and books like Joshua Harris's *I Kissed Dating Goodbye* infiltrated the minds of youth through conferences, Christian bookstores, and teen magazines. I was no exception. The messages I remember hearing around the topic of sex when I was a teenager consisted primarily of three rules: do not engage in sex before marriage, do not masturbate, and do not put yourself in a vulnerable position where you may be tempted to go "too far" with the opposite sex. Where exactly you crossed that line of "too far" was a little vague though, and it often depended on who you asked.

For girls, we had the added responsibility of dressing modestly so as not to tempt the boys to lust. I heard more than once that "guys only want one thing," which intentionally instilled fear into us teen girls so we'd remain virgins until our wedding days. It didn't matter where I turned—whether that was Focus's magazine for teen girls, *Brio and Beyond*, or church youth group,

27

or female mentors like those who influenced the GGG club—
the message was the same. Sex before marriage was bad and sex
after marriage was beautiful, like a switch that flipped from bad
to good on your wedding night.

So it came as no surprise when my thirteenth birthday was
celebrated with a purity ceremony. I was taught that I would be
a better role model for other Christians if I followed the teachings of 1 Timothy 4:12 and "did not let anyone look down on
(me) because (I was) young, but set an example for the believers
in speech, in conduct, in love, in faith, and in purity." Being
pure was not only something I was supposed to want for myself,
it was also an example I was supposed to set for others.

Somehow, thirteen was the magical age that set you apart.
Approaching my teenage years marked the beginning of my
journey from girlhood into being a young woman. To celebrate
this momentous occasion, grandparents, aunts, and cousins
from out of state came to be part of my special day. Family and
friends all gathered together for this coming-of-age ceremony
and pledge of commitment.

Before I took my vow of purity, each person in the room
had their chance to sit beside me and publicly share something
they knew or admired about me. Some recalled special memories, some quoted inspiring Scriptures, and some gave wisdom
and advice for my future. Tears filled the room from precious
moments of nostalgia.

When everyone was done saying their bit, my parents pre-
sented me with a hope chest in which I could store all my hopes
and dreams for the future. This gift undoubtedly pointed to
my wedding day and future family. Already stocked with cook-
books and crocheted doilies, I was to continue collecting my

future dreams and storing them inside for when I settled down and got married. Over the years, things I hoped to use with my some-day family, as well as mementos I wanted to share with them, filled the cedar chest.

Ironically, that chest is now beautifully displayed in the home my wife and I have built together. Some of the items stored in the chest have been brought out and put to use, just as they were intended to, while other keepsakes (like the veil I wore at our wedding) have been carefully stored within. Old dreams have become new memories, even when those memories have turned out to look different than my thirteen-year-old self expected.

*My hope chest that still holds memorabilia from my
childhood along with keepsakes from my wedding*

One of the items that still lie in the bottom of the chest is the Purity Pledge I took that day. Before signing the vow, my parents spoke about the importance of purity and living a life "holy unto God." My dad read to everyone present the pledge I was about to publicly sign.

Believing and waiting for God's best, I pledge myself to be sexually pure until I enter into a marriage relationship, ordained by God, and with the person God has chosen for me. Lord, help me to keep this commandment, so that I may honor You, my family, and my future mate.

"Flee also youthful lusts; but follow righteousness, faith, charity, peace, with them that call on the Lord out of a pure heart."
—2 Timothy 2:22

I find it interesting that nowhere did it say "husband" or "man of God." It simply states "a marriage relationship, ordained by God, and with the person God has chosen for me." I know that was to make it gender neutral and applicable to both sexes, but looking back on it now as a Christian woman married to a Christian woman, I believe that I *have* entered into a marriage relationship ordained by God and that she absolutely *is* the person God has chosen for me.

But it was a long journey before I came to terms not only with my sexuality, but also with how my sexual orientation is embedded in my faith in God. With my entire thirteen-year-old heart, I took the pen in my hand and signed on the dotted line of that Purity Pledge, intending with everything in me to stay sexually pure until my wedding night.

My Purity Pledge, purity ring, and roses from my purity ceremony

My dad then opened the velvet box that contained my purity ring. It was sterling silver with a cross, a heart, and a key signifying that Christ held the key to my heart until the day came for me to be married. On that day, I would join my life with that of my husband in holy union. Pulling it out of its case, Dad looked at me through misty eyes.

"Am," he began, blinking back tears, "today marks the start of a new journey for you—the journey of becoming a young woman. As your dad, I want nothing but the very best for you and I'm so proud of the way you've always put God first in your life. In the years to come, your mom and I promise to stand by you and coach you along as you navigate the many challenges

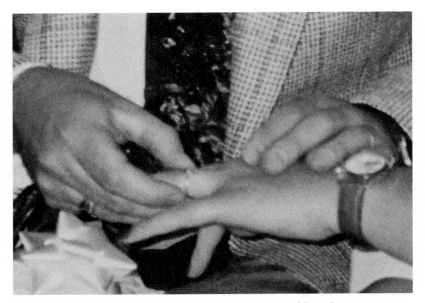

My dad placing my purity ring on my wedding finger

that lie ahead. As you wear this ring, let it be a compass that guides you throughout your life; a constant reminder every time you look at it of the pledge you've made before God, your family, and your friends. I love you, and I'm so proud to be your dad."

He placed the ring on my wedding finger and wrapped his arms around me in a long embrace. Gathering everyone around to pray over me and seal the commitment I had just made, I felt the responsibility before me like a weight on my shoulders.

• • • • •

Throughout my teen years, I wore that ring with pride and every intention of keeping my vow. I took my commitment seriously and planned on fulfilling it. I'd often tell myself that I wasn't dating because I didn't want to put myself in a compromising situation. But the truth was, I really didn't have any desire to date. Even during puberty, I had no interest in boys. Perhaps that should have been a sign to me of things to come, but my naïveté masked reality.

I watched many of my friends go through the exhausting cycle of dating, breaking up, and having their hearts broken, only to repeat the process over again. I thanked God that wasn't me. I convinced myself that I was grateful God had saved me from all that heartache, even when I found myself lonely. I knew in due time, if I was patient and remained true to my vow of purity, God would reward me with my knight in shining armor.

The purity vow cemented in me early on that, according to my family and Focus and God, there was one acceptable way to love. You were expected to keep yourself sexually pure in body, mind, and spirit until your wedding day when you would then give all of yourself to your husband for the rest of your life.

I now have a much different view of the purity culture. For many, I've seen it do much more harm than good. More of a scare tactic for chastity than a doctrine of theology, it addresses deeper issues than just the value of abstinence for the sake of health and fertility. It wraps your entire identity up in your purity and virginity. For many, that has caused great harm in their romantic relationships as they entered adulthood, causing them to get married before they should in order to stay chaste. On the flipside, it has caused great guilt and shame long into what should have been a healthy marriage simply because they didn't keep their promise and were sexually active prior to their wedding night. It also greatly distances them from their relationship with God in the process.

As I've been writing this book, Joshua Harris (author of *I Kissed Dating Goodbye* and a strongly influential figure in the purity movement) has reassessed his views on courtship and dating since he now has boys of his own who are becoming teenagers.[3] When I was a teenager, I had no idea that Joshua Harris was only twenty-one years old when he wrote the book *I Kissed Dating Goodbye*. He was a virgin and had been home-schooled his whole life, just like me. As an adult, it angers me that so many Christian ministries like Focus backed him and jumped on the purity bandwagon because of a guy who was virtually still a kid himself and had no real experience in either dating or marriage.

I'm especially sorry for women, because we've been taught that our virginity is the prize we present to our spouse on our wedding night. If that is lost (due to premarital sex) or stolen (through rape or abuse), then it causes us to feel dirty and used. Convinced that nobody is ever going to want us now, we internalize feelings of worthlessness.

At youth group, my youth pastor used the analogy of a stick of gum. He said that having sex before marriage is like ABC (Already Been Chewed) gum and, with each person you sleep with, you're passing on that stick of used gum and picking up all the germs (or STDs) that come along with it in the process. Each time you sleep with someone, you're also sleeping with every person they've ever been with and, at the same time, creating an eternal tie with them.

---

3. http://www.slate.com/articles/life/faithbased/2016/08/i_kissed_dating_goodbye _author_is_maybe_kind_of_sorry.html.

I'm not denying the value of abstinence, but I do believe it needs to be taught differently. Painting a warped view of sex in the moldable minds of young Christian teens can, and often does, cause lasting harm not only for them, but also for their future relationship with their spouses.

But for me, at the age of thirteen, I knew of nothing else. Purity was an assurance that happiness was in my future. Staying pure was what every good Christian teenager was supposed to do. So with a desire to please God, my parents, and those I respected and admired most, I fell in line.

As I built my hopes and dreams for my future husband and family, one of the first things to go into my hope chest came from a project that Mom and Shaina assigned our GGG group. At an event they called a Legacy Tea, we were to write two letters for the future: one to our future husband, and one to our future child. My letter to my future husband went like this:

My Dearest Husband,

I am writing this letter to you to let you know that I look forward to being your future wife. Even though I am just a young girl now, I truly want God's will in my life, and know he has chosen you for me. I want you to know that from now until I meet you, I will be committed to praying for you and for God's direction in your life. In Psalm 37:4, God tells us, "Delight yourself also in the Lord and He will give you the desires of your heart." These are the qualities I desire to have in a husband.

I desire that you:

- *Love the Lord with all of your heart*
- *Trust in God instead of in worldly things*

- *Show respect to me*
- *Are a good loving father and a wonderful husband*
- *Are a faithful servant and work hard to accomplish things*
- *Have musical talents*
- *Like children and enjoy playing with them*
- *Have blue eyes*
- *Enjoy playing sports*
- *Are sharp and handsome (with no beard and maybe a mustache)*

I would also like you to know that from now until our wedding day, I pledge to keep my body, mind, and heart totally pure so that I can be the best wife for you that God intends me to be.

I love you and look forward to sharing our lives together for the glory of God.

Amber

I laugh looking back at this now. Many of those qualities sound like a scripted version of traits my mom told me were important to look for rather than thoughts of my own. Mentioning sports as important is ironic because I never liked sports. I can only assume it was a common expectation among my peers. And the comment about facial hair, well, we just won't go there!

I wrote this letter on fancy paper, put it in an envelope, and sealed it with a note that said: "Open on Wedding Day." I then placed it, along with the letter to my future child, into my hope chest, locked away with all my other future ambitions and dreams.

I'd like to say I had an inkling about my sexual orientation back then, but I didn't. Words like *gay* and *straight* weren't even a part of my vocabulary. In fact, my knowledge about sex as a whole was quite limited. I knew how babies were made and I knew what sex was, but I also knew that the only time sex was acceptable, was within the context of marriage. Those realities made it extremely difficult to talk about sex at all, especially when an unexpected flashback hit my pre-teen consciousness like a freight train.

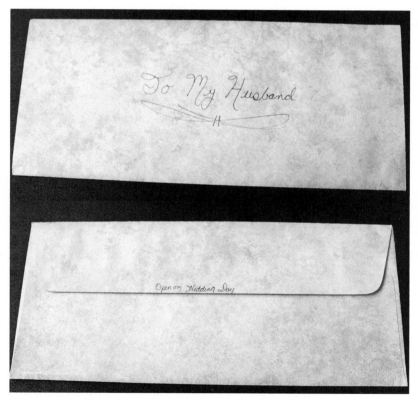

The letter I wrote to my future husband at age thirteen

• • • • •

Around the age of nine, I was on the couch in the family room mindlessly watching a TV show. Whatever show was playing couldn't have been anything graphic since our parents strictly monitored what came across our TV screen. Yet, something I saw suddenly triggered a flashback in my mind to memories I had managed to suppress for several years. Fear overtook me and panic riddled my body as I sat on the couch not knowing what to do. Scared and upset, I crawled behind the recliner in the corner, curled up in a ball, and began to cry. A few moments passed. Then, hearing my tears from the kitchen, my mom came to see what was wrong. Finding me in the corner where I was hiding, she gently brought me out and sat next to me on the couch.

"What's wrong, honey?" she asked, wiping a tear from my face.

Taking a huge emotional risk, I opened up and shared a very intimate moment with my mom.

"Remember when we lived back in California?" I started, trying to communicate through my tears. She nodded.

"Well, sometimes when I played with Steven next door, we would hide in the back of his mom's big van and . . ." my voice trailed off.

She waited patiently, not wanting to put words in my mouth but fearing what may come next. After several attempts, I managed to tell her what had taken place on those days we hid in the back of the van: sexual acts that did not make sense to me when they happened, nor even now when I described them to my mother. Years passed before I was able to piece together that the sexual abuse my neighborhood friend experienced from his babysitter was being passed on to me in those acts.

But as a pre-teen girl, I described to my mom what happened to the best of my ability and waited for her response. She asked a few questions and then, feeling like she had all the necessary information, calmly replied, "Well honey, sometimes these things just happen. It's natural for kids your age to be curious and experiment."

Curious? Experiment? I felt like my mother was blowing off what I had just shared with her, and brushing it under the rug like the family dirt she didn't want anyone to see.

This was a crucial turning point in my childhood development. I didn't realize it at the time, but her comments that day undermined the significance of what had happened and severed a tie of trust between us. Not validating me downplayed my pain and taught me that it wasn't safe to share the deepest parts of my heart with my own mother. In that moment, I realized that how I felt took a backseat to appearances. That was the moment when I began compartmentalizing my emotions and hiding how I really felt.

My mom's reaction that day also had a deeper spiritual impact on my impressionable heart. I began to see God as a works-based ruler rather than as a forgiving, loving father. If I was good, God was happy with me. If I was bad, he was mad at me. Often using guilt as a scare tactic, my parents generated a fearful view of God in my mind. For a sensitive kid like me, this was effective, but also damaging. I got the impression that I had to be perfect in order to earn God's love rather than realizing that God loved me in spite of my mistakes. Trying hard to do everything right, I'd punish myself with cold showers as penance to make myself clean before God anytime I felt guilty over what had happened in that van. Repenting for my mistake over and over until I felt forgiven, I tried to earn my way back into God's good graces.

Over time, the pressure to withhold my emotions built inside me. Feeling alone with my thoughts caused anxiety. But rather than reaching out, I began withdrawing even more within myself. I hid my heart and buried my feelings so that no one could see how I really felt or who I really was inside.

4

BREAKING THE MOLD

Turning thirteen was a monumental time in my life. Not only did I take a vow of purity and make a commitment to abstain from sex until marriage, but I also discovered New Life Church in Colorado Springs. It was a transitional period for me as I entered young adulthood, but it was also a transformative time for my faith. New Life opened my eyes to a whole different dimension of Christianity, and quickly became the place that I spent most of my free time for the next thirteen years.

The first time I ever went to New Life Church service was with Shaina, the co-leader of the GGG group. Pulling into an empty parking space in the spacious lot on the north end of the campus, Shaina held my hand as we walked into a large, teal-and-white building. It looked more like a warehouse than a church. There was no cross or steeple to be found, and it was much larger than any church I'd ever visited.

Following Shaina into the sanctuary, I couldn't believe my eyes. This congregation didn't number in the hundreds, but in the thousands. People filtered in and greeted each other warmly as the clock on the back wall drew closer to 6:00pm. Taking a seat next to Shaina, I tried to wrap my mind around the excitement buzzing around me. It was a level of stimulation I wasn't used to in church. Soon, the pastor, Ted Haggard, took the stage. With reddish hair and a charismatic smile, he greeted the congregation.

"Well good evening everyone! Isn't it great to be in the house of the Lord?"

Following an opening prayer, the worship leader, Ross Parsley, invited everyone to join him as he led out with a full band in an arrangement of "Shout to the Lord."

I was both intrigued and fascinated. In the back of the room, a barefoot lady danced with a ribbon on a wand. In another corner, a gray-haired man shook a tambourine to the beat. I'd been raised primarily in Nazarene churches prior to this, and this presentation of Pentecostal worship was very new to me. Nazarenes are generally very sedentary worshipers, but these New Lifers sang and danced and gave worship their all. They had a contagious joy about them. They seemed to be encountering God in a way that was real and authentic—almost tangible. It ignited a desire in me to know more, and made me wonder why all churches didn't worship this way.

The music continued for a full forty minutes, which was about three times longer than I was used to. But the presence of God in the room was so strong, it was unlike anything I'd ever felt.

"Thank God, thank God, thank God," Pastor Ted exclaimed as he took the stage again following the offering. It was a phrase I learned he was known for.

He proceeded to preach in a fresh way that engaged me. During my earlier years of Sunday school, I learned about Jesus on flannel boards, practiced Bible drills, and sang songs like "Give Me Oil in My Lamp" and "Father Abraham Had Many Sons." Although I felt a connection with Jesus from a young age, this New Life experience was different, and it took my faith to a deeper level. It was no longer just stories from an ancient book; it was words that were alive, active, and relevant to me today. They provided practical applications that gave me tools for daily living.

The relaxed Sunday-evening atmosphere gave the environment in the room a feeling of refreshment for the soul. It wasn't rushed. Rather, it provided space to slow down and breathe. And room to breathe is exactly what I found my heart needing more and more as I entered my teen years.

I returned with Shaina the next week, and the next. Before long, it was my new church home. I dutifully attended the Nazarene church with my family on Sunday mornings so that I could spend my Sunday evenings at New Life. My parents weren't thrilled about the fact that I was going to two different churches, but they allowed it because they could see the life it sparked inside me.

Over the next three years, New Life Church became my home away from home. It was where I longed to be, sometimes even more than my own house. My parents continued to encourage my "walk with the Lord" in our time together as a family, but New Life was where I found my personal relationship with God abounding. It was my safe place, where I could come before God without having to wear a mask of perfection.

I didn't have to put on a show or pretend that I had all the answers; I didn't have to be consistently happy, I could just be me. And I craved that. If home and with friends was where I had to fake authenticity, church and my worship time with God was where I got to embrace authenticity. I could be genuine, transparent, and real because it was just me and God. It was my safe haven. Those early years I spent at New Life are still some of the sweetest memories with God that I have. It laid a foundation for me that ended up carrying me through the years to come.

I don't know what my life would look like today if I hadn't had those years of encountering God at New Life. If all I knew of God were rules and regulations, it would have been much easier for me to leave the religion of Christianity once I came out as gay. A lot of pain was inflicted on me by Christian leaders in the name of God once I revealed my sexuality. So it's quite possible that I would have left my faith altogether were it not for those foundational years. But the time I spent as a teenager at New Life before realizing my sexual orientation, were years of cultivating a deeply personal relationship with Jesus. And in many ways, I believe that's what has kept me following Christ to this day.

I spent countless hours in worship, tuning out the world around me and focusing my heart and life around Jesus. I have dozens of journals filled from endless hours of pouring out my heart to God and listening for that still small voice in return. I attribute much of that to the training that New Life provided and modeled.

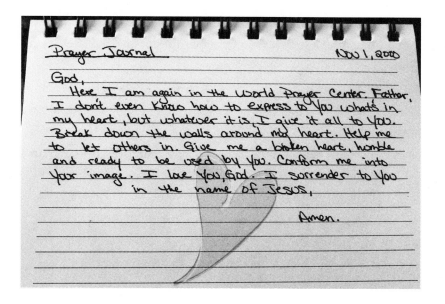

Prayer Journal   Nov 1, 2000

God,
    Here I am again in the World Prayer Center. Father,
I don't even know how to express to You what's in
my heart, but whatever it is, I give it all to You.
Break down the walls around my heart. Help me
to let others in. Give me a broken heart, humble
and ready to be used by you. Conform me into
Your image. I love You, God. I surrender to You
            in the name of Jesus,

                                    Amen.

Wednesdays and Sundays were my favorite days of the week. Graduating from high school at just sixteen, I enrolled in a community college to become a sign language interpreter. The college campus was just opposite New Life, and after class on Wednesdays I walked across the open field to New Life Church. I spent my afternoons in the World Prayer Center on the New Life campus. It was always peaceful. The attractive building was surrounded by flagpoles on the outer perimeter, each flying a flag from the "10/40 window"—a specific region primarily in Asia and Africa known by Christians as being among the poorest in the world and most in need of missionary outreach—and the sanctuary featured floor-to-ceiling windows that gave a breathtaking view of the Rocky Mountains.

The center was open and available for prayer 24/7, and they had a rotating schedule of people who came and led worship during different time slots throughout the week. That's how I met Lena. She led a two-hour worship slot every Wednesday afternoon.

Listening to her, I quickly fell in love with Lena's worship style. The way she sang and played the piano was so raw and authentic. It wasn't at all like the classical music I played to reflect my buttoned-up life. There was something different and attractive about her that I couldn't quite put my finger on. I had to know more.

With my training rooted in classical piano performance, I was never exposed to the world of chord charts and improvisation, but I was intrigued by the way Lena's fingers danced freely. I looked forward to hearing her play every week. Soon, I began telling God that I would do anything to play like her. To me, it was another way to bring together the two things I loved most (music and God). I pleaded with God week after week to unlock that gift inside me. I felt jealous and at times even angry that Lena could play with such freedom when I felt so bound to follow notes on a page.

In hindsight, I see this as a perfect example of how I was feeling about everything in my life at that time. I felt confined, boxed in, restricted, and bound to rules that told me how to live. What I wanted (even though my sexuality was still hiding beneath the surface) was to break loose and be free to live authentically without the need for façades.

When I discovered that Lena taught piano lessons, I convinced my parents to let me switch instructors. They agreed, provided I continued at least some degree of classical work.

What followed was a realization that, as much as I enjoyed listening to Lena play this new style of music, learning to play it myself was challenging. Following rules was embedded in me—not just in my music, but in my life—and figuring out how to follow a new pattern of playing when the whole point was that there was no instruction manual, frustrated me. This world was comprised of endless possibilities and chord progressions. Displaying only a fraction of the diversity that was to come later in my life, playing an improvisational style overwhelmed me and the perfectionist inside me was impatient at my own progress. But my competitive nature pushed me forward until slowly, cracks formed in my classical foundation and began to set me free. My music started to take a shape of its own, as I began playing more like Lena and also writing my own music and leading my own weekly slot of worship at the World Prayer

Leading worship at the World Prayer Center, age sixteen

Center. I felt fulfilled, satisfied, and content with my new way of musical expression.

However, music wasn't the only way that Lena influenced me. While it was her musical style that drew me to her at first, as I got to know Lena I was also drawn to her honesty. Much like her way of playing the piano, Lena didn't live by the rules. She was down-to-earth and practical, and she thrived on knowing God, having fun, and being true to herself. Although I didn't realize it at the time, now I can see that those were all things that drew me to her. As a firstborn child, a people-pleaser, a role model, and as someone whose parents enforced many rules, I was slowly suffocating inside. I desperately wanted to live freely without feeling like someone was watching me or expecting me to be the example. Lena embodied that kind of freedom—she captivated and fascinated me all at once.

There was one additional element that Lena also possessed that no one else in my life did: the ability to make me feel safe. Everywhere I went in life, I felt the need to hold things together. But with Lena, I was given permission to feel my emotions and process them openly. She validated my feelings when everyone else minimized them. When my parents downplayed how I was feeling, or told me to "just trust God more," Lena was the one who saw past my smile and acknowledged my pain. I had never felt so protected and safe.

Our relationship deepened into a mentorship even more when I was spiritually abused at the age of sixteen. A mentally unstable man in town for a prophetic conference preyed upon my innocence and approached me at the World Prayer Center one day. Taking advantage of my trusting nature, he prayed and prophesied things over me that were completely contrary to what I knew to be true. It jostled me and distorted my sense of safety. Disillusioned by the myth that everyone who claims to be a Christian is trustworthy, I lacked the wit and wisdom to set firmer boundaries in a situation of uncertainty.

It was creepy and weird. But it was more than that—something about this man and the way he touched me when he prayed for me made me feel violated. I couldn't explain why—nothing explicitly sexual happened. But something wasn't right. In the weeks that followed the incident, I became hyper-vigilant and paranoid at church, I experienced nightmares, and any mention of prophecy or praying over me caused extreme anxiety. This continued for months.

For years I struggled to explain why it caused me such distress. Eventually, I realized that it undermined my ability to trust in the one place that I felt truly safe—church. It also triggered the same feelings in me that I had experienced as a child when I was molested—exposed, vulnerable, and violated. No matter how hard I tried to brush it off, the prophetic situation ignited such fear in me that it prompted the beginning of my lifelong battle with Post-Traumatic Stress Disorder (PTSD). It was the first in a series of incidents that taught me that church and its leaders aren't always safe.

• • • • •

Lena and I bonded deeply in the months following that encounter. With gentleness and patience, she walked me through the healing process. She could see the fear in my eyes, fear that I didn't know how to communicate, and she allowed me to be scared, to question, and to process without feeling the need to prescribe an instant fix. She'd been there herself, so she understood and empathized with my pain. Her reminders that I was going to be okay grounded me and lent me comfort.

Lena was the first person in my life to ever tell me it was okay to cry. With sixteen years of pent-up emotions, I needed that permission desperately. Fear of what it would look like to actually give voice to my emotions often paralyzed me. But Lena's patience, coupled with her ability to read between the lines and hear what I couldn't say, broke down my walls one by one. Without a doubt, that's why I bonded with Lena so deeply. She met me where I was at, and that's something no one had ever done for me before.

I'm so grateful I met Lena when I did because not long after the prophetic situation happened at church, I was confronted with another uncomfortable situation: I received a diagnosis. And with the stigma I felt because of it, I knew I was going to need Lena's support more than ever to help me through.

· · · · ·

Driving to Lena's for piano lessons one cold January afternoon, my heart was racing from the events of the previous day and the knowledge that came with it. I had accidentally come across a book that my mom borrowed from the library titled *Obsessive Compulsive Behaviors*. Opening to the Table of Contents out of curiosity, I became anxious and uneasy the moment my eyes met the words "Hair-Pulling Disorder" and "Trichotillomania." A knot formed in the pit of my stomach. Reading further in to the chapter, I saw my life on the pages before me.

The book described Trichotillomania (TTM) as a compulsive hair-pulling disorder with traits similar to Obsessive Compulsive Disorder (OCD). It said that the age of onset was typically between eleven and thirteen and can often be associated with a stressful event. While some outgrow it, for others it lasts for life. Symptoms included noticeable hair loss, low self-esteem, significant distress at social functions, and depression.

I was shocked. The book described something I'd been trying to conceal for years. I thought back, trying to pinpoint when this behavior first started. I remembered experiencing some OCD behaviors as a young child, but those faded as I grew older. The hair-pulling, however, started sometime not long before my thirteenth birthday, which fell right in line with the typical age of onset.

I recalled all the ways this disorder subtly influenced my self-esteem. I avoided swimming and trips to water parks with friends out of fear that my makeup might wash off and reveal bald, patchy eyebrows. I dreaded playful makeovers, knowing that allowing someone that close to my face would reveal my missing lashes. This disorder eroded my confidence and made me self-conscious about my appearance.

My perfectionist nature tried to hide and control my hair-pulling at any cost, but almost always left me discouraged at my lack of willpower. Not realizing the chemical and even genetic components until years later, I felt so isolated in my struggle that I often tried to deny it altogether. Even when I journaled about it, I couldn't be honest enough to write "hair-pulling" on the pages. I simply referred to it as "my bad habit." I had no idea that this disorder had a name, and that many others (including some of my cousins) shared the same struggle. I was convinced that it was my own sin. I repented thousands of times, begging God for forgiveness and healing for a behavior I now realized wasn't at all due to lack of faith or a need to trust God more.

On one hand, I felt relieved to finally have an explanation. On the other hand, the thought of having a medically diagnosable disorder terrified me. As estranged as I was from my emotions, I was surprised at the range of feelings I felt bubbling to the surface: shock at the realization of this new label; anger that my mom knew it was a disorder and hadn't told me yet; fear of what this meant for my perfect persona; anxiety about what people would think of me if and when they found out. This was a part of me no one knew, a part of me I didn't want anyone to know. To my knowledge, no one but my parents were aware of my struggle. I had never told anyone, but now I needed to; I needed someone with whom I could process this new information.

Lena was the obvious choice. She was the only person with whom I felt safe enough to talk openly. So I promised myself that no matter how hard or uncomfortable it was for me to expose this embarrassing behavior, I would gather the needed courage to tell Lena at piano lessons the next day.

In the car on the way to Lena's house, my heart raced with anxiety and my knuckles turned white from my grip on the wheel. I hadn't determined exactly how I was going to tell her; all I knew was that I was about to share with her something I had never shared with anyone, and that required a lot of trust.

Arriving at Lena's house just outside of town, I fought to keep my hands from shaking as I sat at the piano, but my anxiety was obvious. Seeing through my façade, Lena wrapped up my piano lesson early, and took me into a back room for some privacy so we could talk.

I took a seat as Lena looked at me inquisitively. But fear of what she would think of me once I showed her what was behind my mask kept the words lodged in my throat. Finally, I simply took the book out of my bag, opened to the correct page, and handed it to her.

Waiting for her to read and unable to hold back my tears any longer, I sat there and cried. I had no idea what the consequences were for allowing someone to see the real me, I just knew that I needed Lena. I couldn't afford to lose her, and I deeply hoped that this new information about a very tender piece of my heart wouldn't cause her love for me to disappear.

"Amber, look at me. I do *not* hate you. I love you very much," she insisted. "You have nothing to be ashamed of. You are beautiful, and I mean that. Whatever going through this looks like, I'll be by your side. I want you to let me know what I can do to help."

I should have known that Lena would respond with love rather than judgment. Her outlook on life was different than my family's. She believed in being who you are and embracing where you are in life, rather than trying to measure up to who everybody wants you to be. She gave little regard to what others thought of her and instead focused her energy in being true to herself.

I, on the other hand, was supposed to represent my family and our reputation as a Focus family with poise and grace. Discovering I had TTM was like discovering a hole in my armor. And telling someone about it was revealing my weakness. I felt vulnerable and, knowing nothing other than the environment in which I was raised, feared the implications of trusting someone with this powerful knowledge.

But Lena quickly dispelled my fears—that she would hate me, that she would abandon me, that she would see me differently now and not want to continue to teach or mentor me because of this new information. Her response quickly disposed all that.

As I left that afternoon, an imprint was made on my heart that would last forever. For the first time, someone had seen the deepest parts of me and wasn't appalled. Lena changed my life that day. The permission she gave me to be flawed and human was so refreshing. I finally felt seen and safe at the same time. It was immensely healing for me. She provided a safety net for me to risk being authentic, and because of it, my worldview changed. For the first time, I learned to value honesty more than the mask.

5

PULLING APART
PERFECTION

When it came to my TTM, my parents did everything they knew in order to help me. My mom found Bible verses to encourage me and wrote them out on index cards for me to place around my room. They prayed with me and for me. And in the years prior to realizing that TTM was a diagnosable disorder, they did everything they could think of (or had heard of) to help at home.

They designed an incentive chart with rewards if I didn't pull for certain lengths of time. While it worked sometimes, it affected my self-esteem even more if I didn't measure up. I felt like I was disappointing them. They also made me wear socks over my hands at night so I wouldn't pull and put Vaseline on my fingertips so they'd be too slippery to grip the hair. It was embarrassing, but I complied. Yet it rarely produced results.

Pulling gave me a sense of calm when I was stressed, but it also made me loathe myself afterward. I'd look in the mirror

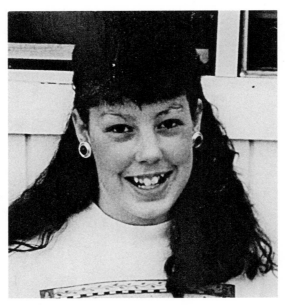

*My patchy eyebrows and swollen
eyelids from pulling, age fourteen*

at my patchy lashes and eyebrows and think to myself, "I am
so ugly."

Often the pulling was subconscious, and I wouldn't even
realize I was doing it until it was too late. At times, I even pulled
in my sleep. Once I started, it was very hard to stop. I hated that
I couldn't control it, and I hated that it made my struggles so
visible. It was embarrassing, and as a result I pulled away from
people, and for years couldn't even look people in the eye.

Once the behavior was labeled as TTM, my parents sought
outside help. They took me to a psychiatrist who coldly asked
me about my behaviors and stress. They took me to a Christian counselor, which in my Christian community held great
stigma—needing counseling was a sign of weakness, a sign

that something was wrong, and good Christians who had Jesus weren't supposed to have anything wrong. But the negative connotation of having a mental health disorder exceeded the stigma of counseling. So my parents found someone knowledge-able in TTM. But our conversations were awkward and felt like part of a formula to simply "cure" me. I didn't trust her. I needed to talk to someone who made me feel safe, like Lena. Faced with a mission to return me to packaged perfection, I found it hard to open up and share with my counselor honestly.

When all those efforts failed, my parents resorted to taking me to see one of our church pastors who specialized in deliver-ance ministry. These meetings took place off-site during the week in the pastor's private office. Arriving with both my par-ents one afternoon, a tall, husky man and his wife prepared me for exorcism. They laid their hands on me, begged God to come, and began calling out my demons of depression, anxiety, and hair-pulling. I felt extremely uncomfortable, not to men-tion terrified.

"Lift your hands upward, Amber."

"Believe in the power of Jesus, Amber."

"Proclaim that you want to be free, Amber."

"Denounce the power these demons have over your life, Amber."

I did want to be free, but the idea that there were demons living inside me was mortifying to me, and this method of attaining freedom was traumatizing. The anxiety I felt over what happened the last time I let a man pray over me only com-pounded my fear. With the palms of my hands facing upward to receive, I tried to be open to God, but I didn't feel safe.

"I rebuke you, spirit of depression, and command that you come out so that Amber can be free in the name of Jesus!" the pastor said with authority in a loud voice.

I managed to hold myself together for the length of the session, but once my deliverance was over, my parents realized that nothing, not even an exorcism, could cure me. They were getting discouraged.

• • • • •

One of the only memories I have of my dad losing his temper was over my hair-pulling. Standing in the kitchen late one night, his patience for my lack of recovery was spent and he exploded.

"Can't you stop?!? Why don't you just stop? Can't you see how horrible you look? Just look at yourself in the mirror! You look awful!" This was the first time I'd ever experienced such an outburst from my dad. His words stung, hurt, and rang in my head for years to come.

Like many teens who are struggling with their parents, I looked to other adults for support and advice. Focus taught that positive role models for your kids were important, and my parents believed that mentoring from other Christian adults was both helpful and healthy. But it was bittersweet for them as I grew closer to Shaina and Lena. It was hard for my mom to see me confiding in her friends rather than in her. But no matter how many times I tried to explain to her how their reactions made me feel, it always seemed to fall on deaf ears.

In hindsight, I believe my parents wanted to help me but didn't know how. At times, I think it frightened them. The things I struggled with didn't add up for a girl with my home-schooled,

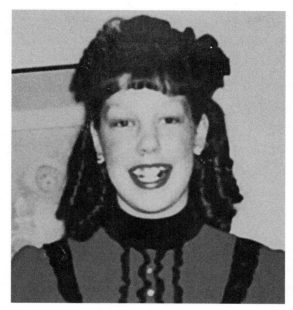

At age fifteen, my thick eyebrows were nonexistent.

Focus on the Family, Christian upbringing. My parents followed all the models, they read all the books, they raised me with all the principles and values that Focus on the Family and James Dobson encourage. They couldn't understand where all this was coming from. So, like any good Christian parent they tried to push me closer to Jesus.

My depression, anxiety, and hair-pulling were the beginning symptoms of my internal struggle with sexuality. I know that now. But at the time, all I knew was that I was different. I tried hard to fit in, but I felt like a misfit everywhere I went.

Being home-schooled put me ahead of all my peers in education, but it also kept me behind socially. I loved the benefit of accelerated learning—it kept me challenged and engaged, which I needed. But the downside was that graduating from high school at the age of sixteen, and having my college degree by eighteen, made it hard for me to fit in and make friends, especially friends my own age. I was sixteen and attending community college, which meant I didn't fit in with the high school crowd, but I also still lived at home and was young, which meant I didn't fit in with the college crowd. I was as mature as all my college classmates, but the youngest person in every group I joined. Often seen as the baby of the group, I hated feeling patronized. It served as a constant reminder that I didn't *really* fit in.

I also didn't relate to my friends when it came to liking and dating boys.

"Isn't Jonathan Taylor Thomas so hot?" they'd ask me as we both looked at a poster of the teenage actor on their wall.

"Oh, I know!" I'd say, just to fit in. But in reality I felt nothing. It didn't interest me the way it did them. Now I can see that what many of my friends felt for boys, I felt for many of my female friends. Perhaps if I had known other gay people or taken sex ed classes in school, I would have had the words to accompany my buried feelings. But because I lacked that, these feelings didn't make sense to me, and my closeted sexuality caused me to feel even more alienated. Unfortunately, it would take another decade for me to finally put a name to my struggles.

· · · · ·

Our reputation as a family grew during my teen years as my dad's work at Focus continued to expand and flourish. In many ways I felt as though I was living in the shadow of my family. At Focus on the Family, I was my dad's daughter; at Green Gable Girls I was my mother's daughter; and as Daniel grew up, he became quite popular at New Life Church, so I became his sister. I was always known by my relation to someone else in my family.

In fact, years after my brother moved out of state and I moved to Denver, I decided to visit a church-plant of New Life in the Denver area. Hoping no one would recognize me, I slipped in just before the service started and sat in the back. I wanted to be somewhere familiar, but I also wanted to be invisible. After worship, we were told to greet those around us. I turned to *one* person and shook their hand, and they looked at me and said,

"Hey, you're Daniel's sister, aren't you?"

I exhaled in defeat.

"Yes, I am," I said with a smile. But I was frustrated. Situations like this made me feel invisible and unable to be seen for who I was apart from my family. Because of this, I often just wore a smile, and took on the problems of others without any safe place to share my own. Lena was really my only confidant during those years of struggle.

But then one day, my very worst fear came true.

• • • • •

Lena and I had just finished another heart-to-heart conversation in the hall after church one night. True to form, she made me feel heard, validated, and safe. Always grateful for the way she made time for me, I gave her a hug as we went to leave, and said, "Thanks for taking the time to talk, Lena. I really do appreciate it."

"You're worth every minute of it, Amber," she replied. "I love you very much!" And with that, she turned and left.

I had no idea that something had snapped inside Lena that night. The next day, she contacted my parents, came to our home, and returned the money they had paid for my piano lessons that month. Then, without even a hug goodbye, she walked out the door, never to speak to me again.

I was shell-shocked. I kept replaying the situation over and over in my mind. Nothing was wrong when she left the night before. Everything seemed fine. So what on earth happened!?! I couldn't make sense of it. Countless times along the way I'd asked her if our talks together were getting to be too much. Each time, she had replied, "No, not at all!" If that were true, then why would she so unexpectedly abandon me? She knew how much our relationship and time together meant to me. She knew how much I needed her. It felt like the ultimate betrayal from the only safe person I had. I was heartsick.

To this day, the only thing that makes sense to me is that she neglected to tell me how she really felt, and in fact was overwhelmed by the weight of what I shared. Perhaps knowing I wasn't always able to trust my parents with the same depth of information, she suddenly became frightened and it caused her to pull away.

Today, I can understand how she may have felt that way. The things I confided in her weren't easy. But it still pains me to think of how she handled it. I wish she had been honest with me when I asked her. I deserved to know and have some warning. She was the person I trusted most, the only one that truly made me feel safe. The only one with whom I didn't have to wear a mask—the only one who would let me cry.

I was perplexed, confused, and scared, but I was also deeply hurt. Lena had promised me that she would be there when I needed her, that she loved me, and that she would stick with me through my troubling times no matter what. Now, overnight, she was gone. In an instant, she had erased herself from my life. Even when I saw her at church, she didn't acknowledge me. I was devastated.

In time, my pain turned to anger, and I decided that if the one person I had finally trusted with my heart was capable of walking out on me, then I wasn't going to trust *anybody*. I completely shut down my emotions. I closed the vault to my heart and locked it tight. I decided I would handle things on my own from now on, and did whatever I could to numb the pain.

*One night, in the midst of unbearable heartache and not knowing what else to do, I picked up a shaving razor, uncovered my right leg, and sliced it across the skin of my upper thigh. It drew blood and I experienced an odd sense of release. It was as if all the pent-up emotions I'd harbored inside spilled out of me along with the blood. I felt both temporarily numb from my emotional pain and temporarily free from it. I quickly realized that I preferred the physical pain on my body to the emotional pain in my heart. It was tangible and I could control it. It was symbolic of what I felt inside—an outward representation of my inner pain. Over time, the blade became my new friend, my secret way of coping. It was never a cry for help; rather, it was my way of surviving the quiet inner agony my heart was bearing. And I shared it with no one.

*Trigger Warning: Please keep yourself safe and skip this paragraph if you feel reading about self-injury may trigger you.

6

GROWING IN THE FURNACE

I was a girly girl, especially when I was young. I enjoyed dolls, tea parties, and playing dress-up. But as I got into my teens, I never felt comfortable about my appearance (especially with TTM), and felt like I constantly struggled to measure up to society's standards.

I never liked wearing jeans, even when I was young. I preferred tights or stretch pants instead. But one day at the store I saw a pair of carpenter jeans in the men's department that looked comfortable. Similar to the hoodie selection that still occupies a large portion of my wardrobe, it felt like a piece of clothing I could cuddle up in and hide inside of.

So I bought them and started wearing them. A lot. Since this was a notable change to my family, my dad decided to comment.

"What's up with those jeans, Amber? What are you, a cross-dresser?" he said with a smirk, half sarcastic, half serious. I shrugged it off with a forced smile, trying to hide how much it hurt.

"What size are they anyway?" he continued, seeing how loose they were. When I told him, he laughed, implying that the size was bigger than anything he'd ever bought. I tried not to show how much it dented my self-esteem. This wasn't the first time I'd heard one of my family members make a condescending remark about LGBT people, but even though I didn't yet identify as gay, this comment stung because it was personal. I already felt uneasy in my own skin. It was another lesson that in my family, it was unsafe to be myself.

*Trying to shield myself from further condescending comments and coupled with the loss of Lena, I remained alone in my pain and continued to turn to self-injury to soothe myself. Like a friend you keep going back to for comfort, even when you know they're bad for you, I knew cutting was wrong. But out of all my coping mechanisms, this one brought the most relief.

*They were mostly surface cuts at first. But like many negative coping behaviors, self-injury required a little more each time to get the same release—more cuts, bigger cuts, longer cuts, deeper cuts. Soon both my thighs were completely covered in long, thin slice marks. Although I tried to save cutting as a last resort, when I did give in, each cut had to trump the last. Relying on my polished poker face to cover my pain with a smile, I knew how to keep my cuts hidden so that no one ever saw them. Showcasing my weaknesses made me feel defeated and vulnerable—like I wasn't strong enough. I hated that feeling.

At the root of it though was fear. Fear of pat answers and being misunderstood. Fear of the underlying message that people

***Trigger Warning:** Please keep yourself safe and skip this paragraph if you feel reading about self-injury may trigger you.

just wanted me to buck up. Fear of being a burden. Fear of being rejected. Fear of being abandoned. Fear of being beyond repair. Fear of feeling even more alone after asking for help than I did to begin with.

Deep inside I longed for someone to hear what I didn't know how to say. I longed for someone to see past my smile and tell me I was safe. I longed for someone to be strong for me, so that I didn't have to. I longed for someone like Lena. But instead, when I'd tell someone how I was doing, I would often get a cliché like, "Well, God will work everything out. Just believe and good will come from this someday, you'll see."

Or, even worse, "Well, I'm glad you're doing well!"

Their lack of empathy caused me to retract and isolate my heart from people even more.

· · · · ·

At church one night, I finally leveled with myself and wrote out the fears I was harboring. As I looked at the page, I saw secrets I didn't even realize I was keeping:

- *I'm afraid that God is disappointed in me.*
- *I'm afraid that nobody is who they claim to be.*
- *I'm afraid to need people.*
- *I'm afraid that nothing good lasts.*
- *Sometimes I wonder why I've never been on a date.*
- *I still want to cut myself and am ashamed because of it.*
- *I go through the drive-through and then sit and eat in my car so people won't know that I'm lonely. Sometimes, I even convince myself.*
- *I'm afraid that I may never be good enough.*

- *I'm afraid to write down my secrets because then I fail to live up to the expectations of others, myself, and God.*

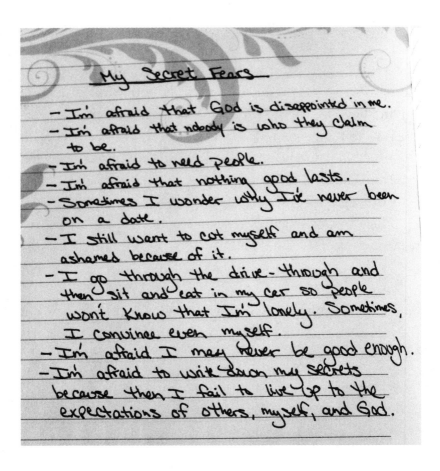

My Secret Fears

- I'm afraid that God is disappointed in me.
- I'm afraid that nobody is who they claim to be.
- I'm afraid to need people.
- I'm afraid that nothing good lasts.
- Sometimes I wonder why I've never been on a date.
- I still want to cut myself and am ashamed because of it.
- I go through the drive-through and then sit and eat in my car so people won't know that I'm lonely. Sometimes, I convince even myself.
- I'm afraid I may never be good enough.
- I'm afraid to write down my secrets because then I fail to live up to the expectations of others, myself, and God.

Bringing my own fears into the light, I could see that my pain was festering. So with hope that it would provide the support I needed, I enrolled myself in an internship program that New Life Church offered for young adults called The Furnace. It was a fifteen-hour-a-week program specifically designed to focus on leadership, discipleship, and prayer.

The expectations in the program were high. They had a no-tolerance policy for smoking, drugs, sex, homosexuality, alcohol, cursing, or for the first semester, even dating. The list of things that we "Must Do" and "Must Not Do" was extensive and we had to signify our agreement by signing a covenant of commitment to these standards for the next nine months—like Christian boot camp.

When I look back at the long list of things required to be a part of this internship, some of the demands seem crazy. As an adult, I can now see how many people outside of the Christian faith would look at the list of obligations and find it ludicrous, even cult-like. But at the time, we were told we were radicals for Jesus. The leadership was strict about accountability and convinced us that seeking God while in this program was the only thing that mattered because we were the world-changers of the next generation. And in Christian culture at that time, buzzwords like "passionate desperation," "zeal for God," and "world-changer" were admirable qualities. Not for the faint of heart, these internships were for the best, most committed type of Christ-followers. Growing up entrenched in this Christian culture, I was used to sacrifice and maintaining good appearances and I wanted to be among those who were in the elite club of "God's favorites."

But I was also in search of healing. Spending time in prayer and worship almost every night gave me the much-needed space I desperately longed for to just sit before God and heal. It intentionally carved out time to just be present and let God work in my heart. I likened it to a metaphorical heart surgery, with me as the patient and God as the Great Physician. Surrendering my pride, I invited God to do whatever necessary to heal my

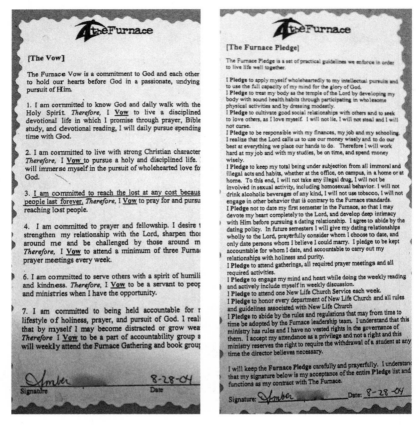

The Furnace Vow and Pledge required to be a part of the internship

brokenness and make my heart whole again, and I committed myself to the process for as long as it took. Those hours of just me and God were precious, even when they were painful.

Several months into the internship, I was encouraged by receiving this card from one of my accountability partners.

> *Amber,*
>
> *When I met you, I was overwhelmed by a sense of Holy purpose on your life. I believe God is going to use you*

to impart the knowledge of God to others who are unable to understand—like a funnel for the Spirit of God.

This is your time, your year, your hour, your moment. Seize it and go after God with all your heart! You are precious, you are beautiful, you are so loved!

Love,

Joy

I've never thrown that card away. Every time I read it, it continues to inspire and encourage me. The fact that she saw purpose in my life even when I was in a painful season spurred me forward and challenged me to keep pressing into the healing process night after night. I experienced much restoration during those months. Taking everything before God and granting full access to my heart, we carefully worked through each piece of brokenness.

I worked hard to learn better boundaries, to not take on other people's baggage, and to trust the right people with my own. I explored what it meant to stand up for myself so that people couldn't walk all over me. I fought for my dignity and worth.

I also educated myself about PTSD. Through my research, I learned that severe trauma physically alters your brain, making it unable to differentiate between past and present experiences. It leaves an imprint on you and makes it difficult to regulate fear and anxiety in situations that are not related (or only remotely related) to the actual trauma. With PTSD, even though the current situation may be totally different than the trauma, it acts like a mirror, flashing you back to that moment with the same intensity as when it initially took place, and making you believe that it's happening all over again.

For trauma victims like me, the fight-or-flight mode often has a third component: freeze. That's exactly what I do. I freeze up while trauma wages war in my mind. Because I have both PTSD and am an internal processor, there are times that I run the whole cycle of PTSD in my body and mind without anyone ever knowing or actually seeing an external clue, like a shackling fear that keeps me captive and silenced. I became so adept at wearing a smile that I was able to hide my PTSD well. Living with this condition as a persistent real possibility and knowing that it could visit completely unnoticed by the public eye, was—and still is—isolating, frightening, and at times debilitating. Retraining my brain as best as I could and becoming aware of my triggers helped me feel more grounded.

This new knowledge coupled with time spent with God brought me leaps and bounds in my process of healing. Slowly, the icy numbness in my heart melted, and freedom returned to my life. I started losing weight, coming off all my anti-depressant medications, sleeping better, and ceasing my habit of self-harm. I was happy, and I felt free. For the first time in several years, the clouds were clearing and the sun was shining through.

The biggest challenge that I still faced was the pain I felt from the loss of Lena. It was like a death, but worse. The person I'd trusted the most betrayed me the deepest. The place inside me that for the first time felt truly loved and safe was abandoned. I didn't know how to let go and move on. I met with her briefly about a year after the falling out in search of some kind of closure. I apologized for whatever part I played in the way our relationship had ended, and she accepted my apology as if I owed it to her, but she offered none in return. My heart continued to ache.

Therapeutic art I created before and after The Furnace

I had to find a way to reconcile occupying the same space at New Life with Lena, even in the absence of relationship. New Life Church may be big, but we often ran in the same circles, which made our interaction hard to avoid. So when challenged at church one day to send a card to someone during the holiday season that we either hadn't spoken to for a long time or that we needed to forgive, I immediately thought of Lena. In one final attempt for reconciliation, or at least healing in my own heart, I mustered the courage to send her a card. It simply said:

Lena,

I was thinking about you during this holiday season and wanted you to know that I hope you and your family have a wonderful Christmas together.

Merry Christmas,

Amber

It was more an act of forgiveness for my own sake than anything else. Then, a couple of weeks later, Lena acknowledged me for the first time in over a year-and-a-half. At church one evening, during the brief window between worship and the sermon when you greet one another, she turned to me from the next choir row over and said, "Thank you for the Christmas card you sent me, Amber. That was very sweet." And she gave me a hug.

Trying not cry, I said, "You're welcome. How are you?"

"I'm well, and you?" she politely responded.

"I'm good."

And that was it. But it was enough. Somehow everything changed in that short encounter. Walls that seemed insurmountable for a split-second didn't exist. It was enough to help me let go and move on.

I often wonder what it would be like to go back and have a conversation with Lena now. Would she be honest with me about what caused her to walk out that day? Would she accept me as a gay Christian woman? I wonder if her faith is on the progressive side of Christianity or if she's conservative in her beliefs. I wonder if she has any idea how much she influenced my life, in both positive and negative ways. Even though many years have passed since then, I still look back to her as an example of how to listen and respond when people share their hearts with me.

· · · · ·

Completing The Furnace was monumental for me, not just because I found closure with Lena, but because it felt like I accomplished something greater than a degree or diploma that year. I accomplished the task of facing my fears, and in return received the reward of healing and wholeness.

After graduating The Furnace, I worked at Focus in several temporary positions. Although I did go through an interview to get the job, my dad's reputation and work history there made it more of a protocol than an actual screening process.

Recently a friend of mine told me that when she interviewed at Focus, they asked her five questions. The first three were about her relationship with God, and the other two were, "What is your stance on abortion?" and, "What is your stance on homosexuality?" Your response to those two questions informed them whether your priorities aligned with theirs.

Focus is a very traditional workplace. As a woman, I was required to wear skirts or dresses with pantyhose daily. We gathered by department for devotions each morning, and a required chapel service for the entire company was held once a month.

Graduating from The Furnace

But despite their conservative policies, they also wanted to be on the cutting-edge of teen culture. So occasionally, on top of releasing articles about being successful in school or developing a relationship with God, they also featured articles focused on self-esteem, eating disorders, or even, self-injury. However, as I began to do my own research, I found very little in the broader Christian culture that addressed some of these more difficult topics. It was as if topics like these were too dark for real Christians to struggle with and should be exclusive to the secular world. But they aren't. Self-injury was quickly becoming the new form of eating disorders in both religious and nonreligious environments and, from personal experience I knew these Christian teens needed someone they could talk to without the stigma of not measuring up or having enough faith.

That's how my passion to reach young women like me began. By this time, I was over two years cut-free and I wanted to find a way to reach those who still suffered in silence. I wanted to obliterate the need for masks of perfection to even exist. I began actively pursuing my dream of using my experience to help other young girls when it came to the more taboo topics in the church: depression, anxiety, sexual abuse, trauma, and self-injury.

While focusing on self-injury was my passion, I wanted to help create a bridge of conversation for all these difficult topics. Today there are so many more resources available on these issues than there were then. At that time there was next to nothing offering guidance out of self-harm from a Christian perspective, and I wanted to change that. I began sharing my story with others.

Several departments at Focus invited me to talk during their devotional hour. The first time was to a group of fifty people. I was nervous to be so vulnerable with people who knew my family so well. I spotted my dad in the audience. He was proud of me for taking this step, but I knew some of the things I planned to say weren't going to be easy for him to hear. Sensitive to the fact that what I shared could reflect on him as a parent, I teetered between apprehension and determination to make a difference.

Over the next twenty-five minutes, I shared my story and battle with self-injury, I talked about what I wanted to do to help others, and I gave them practical tips on why people self-injure as well as common signs to look for. At the end of my talk, everyone applauded my perseverance and thanked me for having the courage to share. Although it was a sensitive topic, they saw it as a victory story. I had overcome self-injury and was now a walking testimony for others.

I then spoke to several other departments at Focus, and talk of my story drifted through the campus. Someone from the media department heard what I was doing and contacted me about doing a TV spot for them on overcoming self-injury. When I agreed, they scheduled a camera crew to come to my apartment and film the spot. They interviewed me, asked some questions about my journey, and shot some footage of things I found therapeutic, like journaling. Soon I became the poster child for teens who have struggled with self-injury in the past but have now found victory in Christ.

• • • • •

At this point in my life, I was an adult and had been out of my parents' house for quite some time, yet, we still kept in touch often. My dad and I frequently ate lunch together while I temped at Focus, and the whole family continued to gather at my parents' house on Friday nights for movies and pizza. While our relationship was superficial in some ways, it was also rich in love, tradition, and devotion to one another.

My mom and I continued to spend girl-time together on a regular basis. Seeing a creative wedding idea in a magazine, we'd dream about my future husband and family. Occasionally, she'd start a sentence with, "One day when you have kids of your own. . . ." These topics allowed us to connect and relate to each other, even though our deeper emotions were usually ignored.

I longed for a husband and family, and I still wore my purity ring with pride. But my heart was growing lonely in a way I hadn't felt before. Nevertheless, I still believed if I followed God's will, in due time he would reward me with my knight in shining armor.

When I told my mom about my dream of helping youth with the unmentionable topics like self-injury, she was proud of me. But it was also clear that the topic made her uncomfortable and she didn't know what to say or how to relate to me. Sometimes silent distance sat between us.

I know it pained my parents to see the struggles I'd gone through, yet they were always good about making a point to tell me how proud they were of my accomplishments. They especially loved that I was actively involved at church, both musically and spiritually. In their eyes, it was much better than what many other teens my age were doing. They also wholeheartedly supported it because being at church not only cultivated my relationship with God, but also kept me inside the bubble of safe Christianity. Or so we all thought.

7

UNEXPECTED
SCANDAL

"Amber, you're a very deep processor; you're independent, you're self-employed, and you have an exquisitely sensitive heart that is possibly compromised by your demeanor and covered up by a smile. You've learned from your parents to shut down your heart, kill your desire, and tolerate disappointment. And now, not only have your parents let you down, but your pastor has as well."

These were the words of the therapist sitting across the room from me. She was right. A sex scandal, drugs, and murder were among the last things I ever imagined having to confront when I joined New Life Church. But that's exactly what landed me back in therapy. The retriggering of my PTSD led me to file with the victim's compensation program that the city of Colorado Springs offered to New Life Church and its members. Filling out the official forms and checking the boxes next to "Victim of Murder/Homicide" and "Mentally Traumatized" as instructed made everything that much more real. For me, it seemed that each new traumatic event was imprinting more easily than the last. That's why I was here—to work through the additional PTSD caused by the recent events at New Life.

New Life Church had been my home away from home for over a decade when the scandal broke out on November 2, 2006: Pastor Ted Haggard had used methamphetamine and had ongoing sexual relations with a gay escort.

Initially, I thought the allegations were ludicrous. "No one in their right mind would actually fall for such a lie," I thought. "It's impossible!" I automatically assumed it was a deceitful attack aimed at undermining Pastor Ted because he was defending Colorado Marriage Amendment 43—an initiative to define marriage in Colorado as a union only between one man and one woman. With the election just a few days away, everyone knew Ted publicly endorsed the amendment. He'd even hung a big banner on the front of the church showing his support.

But at 6am the next day, my phone rang. It was my parents, and I could tell that something was very wrong. With a foreboding tone, they told me it had been confirmed that some of the allegations against Pastor Ted were true.

Denial gave way to shock and disbelief. Ted had always preached transparency and had coined the phrase "There's no such thing as a secret." How could he have held such a deep secret for so long? Disbelief then gave way to a sense of betrayal and deception. It was intense hypocrisy, something I already knew far too well in the Christian church.

My family gathered at my parents' house that day to support one another. Both my brother and I were deeply involved at New Life, so it affected us the most. But my parents were devastated too. This scandal touched the entire Christian community, not only in Colorado Springs, but around the world. Ted Haggard was the president of the National Association of

Evangelicals (NAE),[4] so the news spread fast. Sitting in front of the TV, we watched as newscasters on every channel broadcast the latest information by the hour.

All of Ted's books, sermon CDs, and podcasts were instantly pulled from the church bookstore and website. The man who had started this church in the basement of his home and now had national and even global influence was suddenly erased. It was like he vanished overnight. This is something I've seen happen repeatedly since that day. The gatekeepers—those in Christian radio and retail who decide what to play, promote, and sell—have come up with unspoken criteria that people must meet in order to be promoted. If your music doesn't have enough about Jesus, or if you take a stand for something they deem unacceptable or offensive, like LGBT inclusion in the church, your materials are immediately ripped from the shelves and shunned from Christian bookstores as a matter of protection for the Christian community. That is exactly what happened to Pastor Ted—his legacy and teachings were buried, and we didn't know if we'd ever see him again.

I dreaded that first Sunday following the allegations. It felt like a funeral inside those church walls. Tears, hugs, looks of understanding, and a melancholy atmosphere hung in the air.

There wasn't a dry eye in the place that morning as the church's "head overseer" informed us that Ted was indeed guilty of sexual misconduct as well as of buying meth. Following the by-laws laid out for the church, the group of overseers decided that, rather than working to restore Ted to ministry, this was grounds for permanent dismissal and removal from any kind

---

4. The National Association of Evangelicals is a 30-million-member fellowship of almost forty different denominations nationwide.

of ministry at New Life Church. Ted also resigned his position as president of the NAE. I could do nothing but sit there and accept the horrifying reality of what was taking place, as our service was broadcast live via satellite around the world.

With so many years of wonderful memories at New Life, this seemed like a horrible nightmare. It was surreal to have our cheerful, charismatic pastor whom we all loved suddenly gone, without hope of having any future contact with us. It jolted our entire community. Grappling for hope, at the end of the service we stood in unity and sang, "It Is Well with My Soul."

In the weeks to come, I wrestled with many thoughts and emotions. I began questioning life in a new way. Another layer of my innocence and naïveté had been stripped away and now, not only was I even less trusting, but I was more doubtful as well. The illusion that church was a safe place had been obliterated. I began to question everything—about Ted, about church, about faith, and about life.

Nov. 4th, 2006

My head is still spinning from all that has happened with Ted Haggard these past few days. So many questions fill my mind:

- How long has Ted been engaging in sexual misconduct?
- Have there been others before Mike Jones?
- Does an marriage exist without an affair?
- Are there other discrepancies within the church that I don't know about?
- Who else have I looked up to that I can't really trust?
- If Ted has been buying drugs, have there been times that he's been high when he was preaching?
- What else do we not know about?

My heart hurts, and I know New Life Church will never be the same again.

How long has Ted been engaging in sexual misconduct?

Have there been other men before this one?

Does any marriage exist without an affair?

Are there other discrepancies within the church that I don't know about?

Who else have I looked up to all these years that I can't really trust?

My head spun with questions.

As a church, we had a huge loss to grieve. We grieved the loss of our pastor, founder, and leader. We grieved for our lost reputation. Where we once were known for holiday productions, worship, and CD recordings, we were now known for a sex-and-drug scandal. Our name now carried a new legacy. We grieved the loss of what we knew to be normal.

In many ways, I think the grieving process we went through was similar to the grieving process both my parents and I experienced when I later came out. Suddenly things looked very different than they did before, and we grieved for the loss of legacy, connection, and relationship.

Looking back now, I obviously see the situation with Ted Haggard differently than I did at the time, when my own sexuality was still closeted. Hearing about Ted's sexual misconduct and drug use was a shock, but the fact that it was a gay man added an even deeper weight back then—especially since he was so publicly supporting Colorado Marriage Amendment 43.

I now see it as hypocrisy more than anything else. He was saying one thing publicly and doing the opposite behind closed doors. Any affair is wrong, gay or straight, and using drugs is equally unacceptable for a pastor. But to me, the fact that it was a gay man no longer gives it the added anguish that it used to, other than the deception it exposed.

There's another part of me that is sympathetic for Ted. He climbed the political and evangelical ladder so high and held so much power that he no longer had anyone to confide in. It certainly doesn't excuse his double standard, but it's a prime example of what can happen when we fail to live authentically.

Ted has since started a new church in Colorado Springs and in the process of writing this book, I decided to go and visit. I didn't know what to expect, but what I found felt like a travel back through time. In so many ways, he was the exact same person I'd always known. He's still married to his wife and still has the same charismatic smile. He still uses many of the same phrases he did twenty years ago and still seems to have the same belief system he always did. A piece of me hoped I'd discover that he was LGBT-affirming, but that wasn't the impression I got. The way he preached made it clear that his theology hasn't evolved, even after everything he's been through.

· · · · ·

New Life Church, Ted Haggard, and what became known as "The Scandal" continued to make headlines for months. The persistent new revelations became exhausting, and over time I struggled just to get myself to church. I never knew what piece of traumatizing information would be thrust at me next. I was walking on eggshells, holding my breath.

For years I'd gone to church alone, worshiped alone, sat alone—it never bothered me. I wasn't there to socialize, I was there to meet with God—it was my time to unplug from life and re-center. But as anxiety became the emotion related to

Newspaper headlines after the scandal broke out

all things church and my PTSD compounded with each new trauma, I became unable to go to church without somebody else going with me. Months of continued trauma made church a burden rather than an anchor. I thought I was helping myself by forcing myself to go, but now I realize I was continually putting myself in a traumatizing situation. I still struggle to go to church alone to this day.

By August of the following year, a new senior pastor was elected. We hoped the dust would finally begin to settle so we could return to a sense of normalcy. But much sooner than any of us expected, tragedy struck our church once again.

• • • • •

I was at home on Sunday, December 9, 2007, when tragedy hit New Life Church for the second time. My phone rang and my mom's panic-stricken voice on the other end asked, "Where are you? Are you at church?"

"No, I'm at home. Why?"

"Stay home and don't go anywhere!" she replied. "There's an active shooter at New Life and your brother is still in the building!"

I froze. This call reminded me of the time my dad was trapped inside the Focus on the Family headquarters with a live shooter back in May of 1996. Kerry Steven Dore, who had been injured as a result of a fall while working on the construction site of Focus's main building in 1992, was holding four hostages in the lobby with a handgun and what he claimed were explosives strapped to his back. The phone rang at home.

"Honey, I don't want you to panic," my dad told my mom, "but I'm still inside the building." Assuming the sirens were simply a routine drill and being under a tight deadline, my dad didn't evacuate when the alarms sounded. By the time he was notified that there was a real emergency, it was too late. He was trapped in his office and had to wait it out. Thankfully the hostages were all released after ninety minutes of negotiation and Kerry surrendered to the police by 7:15pm that night. No one was hurt. But that was not the case at New Life Church in 2007.

Live coverage filled every station with breaking news: the parking lot was filled with police cars, SWAT teams, helicopters, fire trucks, and ambulances. My phone immediately started ringing with people checking to see if I was safe. Some were friends from other churches, some had just escaped the New Life building themselves, and some still had family inside.

Soon, Daniel called. He had fled the building and was safe, but he had missed encountering the gunman, Matthew Murray, by only two minutes.

Twenty-four-year-old Matthew Murray had attacked the Youth With A Mission training center in Arvada, CO, in the early morning hours of December 9th, killing two and wounding two others before escaping. He arrived on New Life property later that same morning, thirty minutes after the second service dismissed. His trunk carried an assault rifle, two handguns, smoke bombs, and 1,000 rounds of ammunition. He was

Newspaper headlines after the
shooting at New Life Church

planning for mass destruction. After loading up, he killed two sisters in the parking lot and wounded three others before being shot by a member of the church's security team.

Even after they confirmed one shooter dead, it took hours for them to sweep the building to make sure there weren't any hidden shooters or bombs. The entire campus was locked down the rest of the night and for several days following as the investigation continued.

Wednesday evening, another Family Meeting was called. These Family Meetings had come to make my stomach churn with the painful information they had entailed over the past year, but this night carried a new weight and a fresh level of grief. Driving on campus that night, I saw that media flooded the parking lot with satellite dishes and cameras much like they had just after the news about Ted Haggard broke out. Suddenly, my heart was racing, and I felt myself starting to panic. "I can't do this again," I thought. With only thirteen months between the scandal and the shooting and all that had happened in between, it was overwhelming.

After trying hard to calm myself, I mustered all my strength and went inside. That night we sang Jon Egan's "Overcome" in solidarity, declaring the words of Revelation 12:11, "And they overcame, by the blood of the Lamb and by the word of their testimony. And they did not love their lives so much that they were afraid to die" (NKJV, NLT).

It was one of the most powerful moments of corporate worship I've ever experienced. In the midst of such heartbreak, thousands of voices determined together to press on.

Although I didn't personally know either of the two girls who were murdered that week, New Life focused on being a family, and we corporately grieved the loss of the two sisters. We also grieved the loss of safety in a place we considered a refuge.

. . . . .

I tried my best to move forward with my ministry plans to help young women despite all that I'd experienced at New Life over the past year, but it was hard. I felt drained and didn't think I had much to give. In time, I found someone online who had ministry plans similar to mine, and she connected me with a woman who self-injured named Brooke. Like me, Brooke had been through a lot in her life, and we bonded over our similarities. I took her under my wing and listened to her, encouraged her, and supported her in her journey through self-injury. Before long, Brooke planned a trip to visit me and consider an internship at New Life. I was excited to be finally putting my words into action and seeing this dream come alive. But I never, *ever* expected the turn my life was about to take because of it.

8

FINDING LOVE, BUT
IN THE WRONG PLACE

If someone had told me ten years ago that I'd one day be writing a book advocating for LGBTQ people in the church, I would have scoffed and said they were crazy. I certainly would *never* have believed them if they took it a step further and told me that this theme would be the very definition and story of my *life*. My Focus on the Family upbringing had taught me that the LGBTQ community were basically the archenemy of Christianity and were responsible for destroying the family unit. It was the furthest thing from my mind if asked to describe myself. I was a good girl, a people-pleaser, a goal achiever, a dream chaser. What I did *not* dream was that someday, I would break all those rules. I never dreamed that I would be living outside of the box. That was for rebels.

But then something changed. Sitting in a plush brown chair in the private office of my women's pastor, Nadia, I reflected on what had gotten me to this place. Waiting for her to arrive, I retraced my steps from the time that Brooke and I first met.

• • • • •

It was only five months earlier that Brooke had come to live with me. It seemed so much longer than that. It felt as if we'd known each other for years. When she came for her first visit in December, we bonded instantly. Then, when she applied and was accepted for a New Life Church internship, she asked if she could live with me, and I said yes.

I felt a deep sense of purpose, complemented by compassion, empathy, and love for her. I thrive when I feel needed and useful, like I am making a difference. So for me, having a girl who was struggling with self-injury stay in my home while on her path to healing, was like winning the golden ticket. I put much of my life on hold and poured my time (and money) into her, stopping at nothing to make her feel like an important part of my life, my home, and my family. I desperately wanted her to belong.

My relationship with Brooke changed over time. She moved in as my roommate, and I was her mentor. But we also became best friends. I can't deny that her admiration for me gave me a deep sense of self-worth and fulfillment. She needed me. I was making a difference.

I was only a few years older than Brooke, but if you measured us by maturity level, we were decades apart. I watched as my cozy little apartment morphed into a dwelling clearly inhabited by a teenager. Brooke was nineteen, but with her Teenage Mutant Ninja Turtle trash bin, her brightly colored light-bulb shades on her five-pronged floor lamp, and her stuffed animals, you would have thought she was much closer to the beginning of her teenage years than the end of them.

I let go of control as best I could, which is not easy for a control freak like me. Instead of getting frustrated, I tried to find joy in her childlike nature. With the purest of intentions, I strove to give her the things she'd been deprived of in her youth. In my opinion, every girl deserves to feel safe and loved at home. Brooke had lost her childhood to abuse and neglect, and I tried to give it back to her. I infused my little home with the traditions around birthdays and holidays that made my own childhood special, hoping to re-create those experiences for Brooke. Brooke's mother told her she was a devil child and that she wished Brooke had never been born; I wanted to instill in Brooke a sense of self-worth and value.

Instinctively, I knew there was something unusual about the nature of our relationship, though I wasn't sure what. I just knew that it didn't fit within the confines of that little box we Christians were expected to live inside.

I tried to not let other people's opinions hold weight when it came to how I interacted with Brooke, but that was hard. I had to make an intentional effort to dismiss my need for other people's approval and instead, refocus my attention on the mission at hand, which was to love Brooke as best I could.

While caring for Brooke was both physically taxing and emotionally exhausting, it was also rewarding. I saw her experience love and safety, and I clung to those moments as my reason for continuing to invest in her. But I was also guilty of letting that taint my view of some of the deeper, more troubling behaviors Brooke displayed.

I ignored the warning signals that told me I was in over my head: the controlling texts from Brooke asking where I was and what I was doing; the manipulative behavior, micromanaging my time so it was spent only with her; the frequent threats of self-injury and suicide that came from behind locked doors and kept me deeply concerned and on edge. I dismissed these behaviors by telling myself that God was using me to bring her to a better place. But the truth is, we were both co-dependent. I needed to feel useful, so I poured my energy and love into her. She needed to feel safe and valued, so she soaked it up. It was the perfect storm. It drained me, but stubbornness, determination, and resolve to not fail at this assignment from God kept me pushing forward long past the time when I should have asked for help. I wanted to be the hero. I wanted to save Brooke from her past and be the one who aided her to whole-ness. Our unhealthy tendencies kept us mutually dependent on one another for success and fulfillment.

Meanwhile, lack of dating experience and—let's be hon-est, lack of life experience—kept me naïve and oblivious to the fact that other bonds were forming between us. When she asked me to sing to her, I felt like a nurturer. When she asked me to hold her, I felt like a caretaker. When she left her own bed for mine in the middle of the night, I told myself that I was giving her the love she never received. I was good at compartmentalizing.

My own innocence kept me from recognizing the obvious, and because of that, I was completely unprepared for what hap-pened next.

· · · · ·

It was a Tuesday afternoon and we were lying on the bed in Brooke's room having a heart-to-heart conversation. After Brooke shared her current struggles, I reminded her again that she was safe in my home, that I loved her very much, and that I wasn't going anywhere. In fact, my words to Brooke probably sounded very much to her the way Lena's words once sounded to me: comforting, protective, safe. I remembered how much Lena's willingness to listen meant to me and wanted to provide the same opportunity for Brooke. I promised myself that I would never walk out on Brooke the way Lena had walked out on me. No matter how hard it got, I was determined to remain a faithful ally and supporter in her life. But because I failed to set more appropriate boundaries early on, in the midst of the safety of our heart-to-heart conversation that day, the unspeakable happened.

Suddenly, the tone of the conversation shifted. Affection gave way to a different emotion, one that stirred underneath the surface. Moving in closer, Brooke looked deep into my eyes. Then, with a longing greater than a familial bond, she leaned into me until her lips touched mine with a sensual kiss.

I froze. It lasted only a moment, but it was a defining moment. Quickly backing away, we looked at each other wide-eyed and silent, in shock over what had just taken place. My head was spinning (in more ways than one), but I tried to stay in control. Brooke seemed to do the same. I couldn't tell if she was truly shocked the way I was, or if she only pretended to be and had secretly been thinking about this for some time. Either way, I knew this couldn't be happening. Or shouldn't be.

· · · · ·

That's what brought me into Pastor Nadia's office. I felt the need to talk to my college pastor and ask for guidance. I listened to the clock on the wall tick as I waited. It was about half the speed of my nervous heartbeat. Finally, the door across the room opened and Pastor Nadia walked in.

"Hey Amber, how's it going?" she said with a smile as she took a seat in the black office chair near her desk.

Notorious for appearing much more calm and put together than I actually feel inside, I returned the smile and replied, "I'm fine, how are you?"

Struggling to get to the reason for my visit, I began explaining to Nadia the series of events that had led me to her office. Trying to justify all I had done, I carefully laid the foundation to make sure Nadia would understand why Brooke came to live with me and what my intentions were in having her in my home. I didn't want to appear as messed up as I felt. I decided that calm and composed was the tactful way to approach this situation.

Finally, I told her about the kiss, but I was quick to assure her that it had only happened once and that Brooke and I had talked about it in detail and were sure that if we simply established clearer boundaries, we could move forward in a healthy manner from here. All I needed was for Nadia to validate my already well-thought-out (and very in-control) plan.

"Amber, because I love you and care about you, I need to speak the truth to you in love. This relationship isn't healthy. You talk about the two of you like you're a couple," she said solemnly. "She needs to move out immediately."

Move out?! I felt so misunderstood. I wasn't in love with Brooke. It had only happened once! It was a mistake! I was *in control*! Anger and frustration surfaced as I left, feeling even more confused and discouraged than when I walked in. I wanted to control the conversation, to convince Nadia that the incident was no big deal. I wanted her to understand my intentions and be empathetic. I wanted her to agree that this could be resolved. I wanted her to believe in me.

But instead, the thing I feared the most, is exactly what happened. My mistake was considered a sin by my pastor. And not just any sin, but the worst kind of sin: homosexual sin. Brooke and I were now seen as dirty, tainted, and stained. As much as I hated feeling misunderstood, I hated this judgment even more. It was as if that one kiss now defined us as "struggling homosexuals" in Nadia's eyes. That messed with my desire to maintain appearances. My image of perfection was tarnished.

And even more infuriating than the conversation itself was that Nadia spoke with one of Brooke's church mentors about what had happened. Trust was broken, and once again I felt unsafe at church. It was as if things said in confidence were only kept in confidence to the degree that the person in leadership felt comfortable. Once it crossed the line into something difficult or sticky—something that was more shades of gray than black-and-white—they felt they had the right to disclose it to someone else to ease their conscience and measure of responsibility. Repeatedly disappointed by people such as Lena, Ted Haggard, and now Nadia, I began to distance myself, both from church and from those in church leadership.

The only positive advice we received about what happened came from Brooke's counselor back home. She was a Christian counselor, but was also equipped with a professional degree. She told Brooke not to run from the situation, but to stay and work it out. I was relieved. Finally some sound advice that resonated with what my heart was telling me to do. We talked, we established boundaries, and I pulled back from the affection I was giving her to keep from blurring the lines. I was determined to make this work.

But despite my attempt at willpower, it wasn't long before that willpower gave way to chemistry and pent-up emotion, and we kissed again. The kiss was longer this time, more intimate; not passionate, but slow and sensual. Those few moments were so beautiful and amazing that I didn't want to let them go. I'd never felt anything like it. My whole body came alive and I experienced a type of love I'd never felt before. In shock the first time we kissed, I denied myself that pleasure the first time around. But this time, kissing Brooke brought a deep, inner joy I had never known.

Then came the guilt. I knew that I shouldn't feel this way, no matter how beautiful it was—at least not with Brooke. Kissing another woman was forbidden. Not only that, but I was supposed to be Brooke's role model. Although I didn't initiate the intimacy, I was also unable to stop it. I didn't know what to do. My mind and heart contradicted each other, and I was unsure which to follow. Confusion and conflict worked its way through my body, mind, and soul.

In the coming weeks, we both realized what we had been trying so hard to deny—there was a deeper connection and love present than that of just friends. Our relationship began to shift.

We struggled in turmoil over the complexity of the situation. We couldn't deny the chemistry forming between us, but we couldn't escape the shame either. Guilt haunted our relationship. Yet, when we gave in to temptation, there were moments of pure joy unlike anything either of us had ever experienced.

"How can something that feels so right, be wrong?" we asked over and over together. It just didn't make sense. When we were together, we were so happy. How could happiness be bad? During this time, my joy was so evident that my dad even commented, saying I looked happier now than he'd seen me in a long time. Gulp. I couldn't deny it. I was definitely happy, but not because of something that would make him proud.

. . . . .

Kissing led to experimenting, which led to more than kissing. It started to awaken things in me that my sheltered body didn't even know existed. Up until then, the sexual nature of my body had been quite foreign to me. It cheated me in that way, keeping facts hidden about my femininity that were common knowledge to those around me. Now, new things were coming alive. Still, I fought them, wrestling the roller coaster of this forbidden love.

After several months of struggle, Brooke did what comes most natural to people with a background of abuse and neglect: she went into fight-or-flight mode. I wanted her to stay. I was still convinced we could face this head-on and work it through. Or, dreaming for the impossible, that maybe we might even actually have the potential of building a relationship together. Desperate for a way to make things okay, I even took the risk of speaking these dreams aloud to Brooke. But, overtaken by guilt and fear, Brooke made an impulsive decision to leave for the August kickoff of a different internship program in Michigan. She threw all of her stuff into her Toyota Corolla, and overnight, she was gone.

A flurry of emotions overtook me: devastation, confusion, hurt, overwhelming guilt, and a deep inner sadness—all feelings that I could share with no one because of the latent knowledge that our relationship was detestable in the eyes of God. I tried to console myself by believing that maybe Brooke's decision to leave would be what really helps her turn the corner and come into true healing in her life. We tried to navigate this bumpy road with occasional phone conversations, but got nowhere.

Despite the chaos, I was bound and determined to keep a promise I'd made earlier in the year to take her to see her dad's grave for the five-year anniversary of his death. She had lost enough in her life and I knew she needed this.

We made a long weekend out of it and both agreed ahead of time to abstain from anything sexual while we were there. I was resolute in my determination to keep things platonic, or so I thought.

Lack of romantic experience kept me from realizing that distance does indeed make the heart grow fonder. Seeing each other after nearly two months apart provoked a wave of passion that overtook us when we reunited at the airport. I wrestled, trying to suppress those feelings and stay true to our agreement. But the tension was obvious.

After months of internal wrestling against something that felt so right, in the bed and breakfast room we shared that night, I decided to stop fighting so hard against this desire to love that ran so deep. I knew that sooner or later, I was going to have to face my fear of this fatal attraction. Putting my mind on pause, I decided just once, to put perfection aside and allow my heart to lead the way.

When the sun went down and bedtime came, I lowered my emotional guard as we both crawled into a shared queen bed. But before turning off the light, I looked at the purity ring on my finger, a symbol that had carried me for the past ten years. I was aware of what it represented, but was also aware

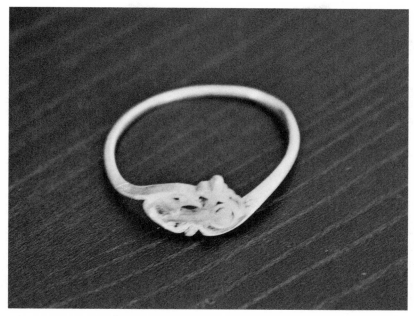

The purity ring I took off that night in the bed and breakfast with Brooke

that something deeper was going on inside me than just routine romantic attraction. I needed to figure out what it was. Knowing full well what I was doing and what it meant, I slipped the ring off my finger. Setting it on the nightstand beside me, with my heart open and my body vulnerable, I took once last glance at it, and with that, reached over, and switched off the light.

9

THE AFTERMATH

Two years ago, my wife and I purchased and moved into our first home. Boxes left untouched in storage for years now begged for my attention. I knew I needed to go through them, but they stared at me for weeks before I found the courage to actually open them up and see what was inside. When I finally did open them, many mixed emotions surfaced as I found baby clothes I had once worn, dolls I'd once played with, and books I'd once read. Half of me was thankful my mom and I had kept these things all these years; I look back on many of them still with great fondness and nostalgia. The other half of me felt conflicted and unsure how I was supposed to feel. This huge part of my life—of family traditions, of holiday memories, and of intentional legacies—are all things that have since been robbed from me. It was a painful reminder that I may never get to experience some of those moments with my family again. Moments of joy and moments of grief arrived on each other's heels in rapid succession. It was almost like these events had taken place in a totally different life: the life I had before I lost everything.

The day I went through my hope chest was an emotional one, the same hope chest my parents had given me at my thirteenth birthday party—the party at which I'd committed myself to sexual purity until marriage and was given the ring by my dad to wear until I met my future husband. Going through each item one by one, as I neared the bottom, lying against the cedar floor of the chest, I found my purity ring. Dark and tarnished, it immediately took me back to that night at the bed and breakfast with Brooke when I took it off forever.

· · · · ·

I intentionally gave Brooke my purity that night. In hindsight, she didn't deserve it. But I made a decision, assuming both its risks and consequences. In some ways, I regretted it deeply. The shame and remorse that followed me afterwards felt completely suffocating at times. But in other ways, I didn't regret it at all. I loved Brooke. I wanted to know her without limitations. And honestly, I'm not sure what else would have catapulted me into my journey of discovering my sexuality, had I not taken that risk. Regardless of regret, that night we spent together marked me for life.

It's a night that would have been steeped in beauty, had it not been tainted by shame and the belief that what we were doing was wrong. I tried hard to silence the condemning voices in my head as we rustled beneath the sheets that night. I wanted to be in the moment, because the truth is, if I could put shame aside, the moment was beautiful. It was perfect. It was love at its most passionate. So I did my best to let go and give her my all. It was freeing to finally give in to temptation. I felt relieved in a way. We had fought against this pull of forbidden love for months and finally, that night, I made the conscious decision to stop fighting.

Following our weekend together, Brooke returned to her internship program in Michigan. We had several follow-up conversations about what that weekend meant for her now that she was back in the program. Should she be honest and tell somebody? Or should she keep it a secret? Having gone through my fair share of internships, I knew that keeping secrets from your leaders was never good. But I also knew that telling them the truth would get her kicked out of the program. There was rarely wiggle room for forgiveness in those types of internships. You go in knowing what's expected of you, and if you don't measure up, you're out.

I knew I couldn't tell her what to do. I certainly wasn't going to tell her to lie to her leaders. So instead, I encouraged her to think about what she wanted in the long run. But it wasn't long before guilt got the best of her and convinced her to confess. She was, as predicted, instantly kicked out of the program and sent home. Sexual behavior of any kind while in the program was unacceptable, but homosexual behavior was completely forbidden. Soon thereafter, she showed up on my doorstep, asking for a second chance at living with me. I hesitantly said yes.

Having had my heart broken the first time Brooke left, I was reluctant to let her live with me again. But part of me wanted to make things right by attempting to go back to the way our relationship was when we first met—back to the friend/mentor status. I thought maybe if we could do that, then it would be like none of this other sexual stuff had ever happened. But I knew backpedaling from sleeping together would be a hard line to draw. I wanted to believe that we were strong enough. Looking back, I realize I was only kidding myself. We loved each other, and being roommates or friends just wasn't going to happen.

I did wonder if we could actually be in a romantic relationship with one another. I was discouraged by the marriages I saw around me during that time. Even with organizations like Focus on the Family emphasizing the importance of marriage and the family unit, it seemed like almost everyone I knew, regardless of age had gone through an affair or divorce. With divorce statistics being just as high among Christians as they are among the population at large, I was not optimistic about a lasting marriage to the someday-husband that I had dreamed of all my life. So, if I already knew I loved Brooke, wasn't it better to be with someone I loved, even though she was a woman, instead of hoping for a fantasy that may only break my heart, if it ever even came true? But that was an unrealistic pipe dream and Brooke and I both knew it. According to our Christian beliefs and upbringings, being in a real romantic relationship with each other was not an option.

It only took three short weeks after she returned to live with me before guilt ate away at Brooke enough for her to flee a second time. But this time, she decided to pay a visit to my parents on her way out. She went to my parents' house the night before she left and outed our relationship to them. Then, once again, she disappeared.

· · · · ·

My parents showed up on my doorstep at 6am the next morning, texting me just before they arrived to say they were on their way over. I knew this wasn't good. Deep down I desperately hoped that they'd arrive bearing hugs of parental love and understanding. I needed a good cry after all this. I was only twenty-four after all, and I longed for someone to tell me that everything was going to be okay. But instead, they stormed in, barely making eye contact with me and sat down, ready to interrogate.

"Has this happened before? How long has this been going on, Amber? How old is she?" they fired, insinuating that this had gone on the whole time Brooke and I knew each other, or worse, that she was underage and I could be convicted of having sex with a minor. It hurt me to the core. Nit-picking through my past, they searched for a point on which to pin the blame. Their long list of questions implied that I'd been hoarding this dirty secret from them for years and manipulating them to believe that my hair-pulling, anxiety, and need for counseling all stemmed from other places, when really *this* was the root of my struggles. In hindsight, I now believe that my closeted sexuality was the root of those struggles, but I certainly was not conscious of that at the time.

I assured them that this situation was just as much of a shock to me when it happened as it was to them when they found out. But I could see in their eyes that they struggled to believe me. I was humiliated and ashamed. The Focus on the Family teachings I was raised on made it clear that traditional marriage (between one man and one woman) was the only marriage that the Bible supports. Divorce was wrong, living with (or having sex with) someone outside of marriage was wrong—and homosexuality was *really* wrong. James Dobson taught that gay people were a threat to traditional marriage in statements like, "If traditional marriage is not the law of the land, the institution of the family will cease to exist." Clearly, my actions were unacceptable, especially for a daughter with the perfect Focus upbringing—and a daughter of a Focus employee no less!

My parents were ashamed, disheartened, and embarrassed by me. I had let them down and failed to uphold the reputation of our family. It was obvious that they were deeply concerned for how this would affect our future. Even though I had begun questioning some of the beliefs taught to me growing up, I wasn't ready to admit that yet. Looking through the lens of the teachings from my Focus upbringing, punishment was what I deserved. Yet, what I really wanted was empathy and understanding.

I blinked back tears, attempting to hide my own disappointment and pain. I tried to buck up and accept their rebuke, but I was broken and afraid.

My parents ended the meeting by saying, "Don't *ever* tell anyone about this, because if you do, it will ruin your reputation forever." Then without even a hug goodbye, they left.

First I was scared, then I was interrogated, and now I was alone.

I've often wondered if it was really my reputation they were worried about or their own. Perhaps they were concerned that my dad's long-term position at Focus could be in jeopardy if it got out. But in the heat of the moment, it didn't seem to matter whether it was my reputation on the line or theirs. We were still a family unit. The actions of one affected all. This theme had always been emphasized in our family. More than once growing up my mom had told me, "What you do reflects on us." So naturally I felt obligated to keep this secret out of duty to my family name.

I was overwhelmed with confusion and fright. And so, like the good, people-pleasing, rule-following daughter I had always been, I did what they said and didn't tell a soul. I used my skill of compartmentalizing to stuff my emotions deep down inside where they could hide forever, and never spoke about it to anyone.

I also made an inner vow to myself that day that I couldn't cry. I wasn't allowed to cry. I didn't deserve to cry. The pain this time was my fault. I had screwed up. Therefore, I didn't have permission to grieve. I deserved what I got, and for the next ten excruciating months, that inner vow kept me silent.

· · · · ·

So many feelings and questions bombarded me in the months following that conversation with my parents. Having a relationship with a girl was, in the eyes of my family, the ultimate form of failure. Not only had I broken the vow I made at thirteen to stay sexually pure until my wedding day, but I did it with someone of the same gender—something I'd been taught that the Bible completely forbids. And to top it off, it wasn't just any girl; this was a Christian girl whom I was supposed to be a role model for. The shame I felt polluted how I thought about myself for months.

My virginity was something I had always wanted to save for my husband. I was convinced that no godly, Christian man was ever going to want me now that I'd given that away. And even if I were able to find a man who was gracious enough to overlook it, I didn't even know what that would look like. Would I still get to wear white on my wedding day? Would I feel special like I'd always dreamed? Or would I walk down the aisle feeling stained by my past and knowing everyone else would also see me that way, if they only knew?

And what was I to say to that some-day husband? "Here's my purity ring. I'm sorry. I tried." I was supposed to give him that ring in exchange for my wedding band. Now, that was a gift I no longer had to give. Of course, for girls like me, the Christian cliché was, "You can become a recycled virgin."

I remember thinking, "Recycled, my ass. Recycled meaning previously used, smashed down, and put back together from garbage."

That's how I felt: like used garbage. The purity ring had been a symbol of my desires and beliefs all my life. Now it was in the bottom of my purse, the tarnished silver serving as a constant reminder of how soiled I felt inside. I knew I could never wear it again—I didn't deserve to. Yet I couldn't bring myself to throw it away either.

I'm sure my parents noticed that I wasn't wearing it anymore, but they never said anything. It was further proof that I could never be the perfect daughter they longed for. Our family was flawed because of me. I was the black sheep.

*Without being able to talk to anyone about my pain, it didn't take long before I turned back to the very thing I'd sworn never to do again: cutting. After almost five years clean, I relapsed, and hard. I began cutting not only on my thighs, but on my forearms as well. I graduated from shaving razors to a utility knife, each time cutting a little more than the last, until a sense of release finally washed over me. As if that weren't enough, I also took up rubber bands as a new form of self-injury. Sliding the thick band around my forearm, I'd pull it back and

---

*Trigger Warning: Please keep yourself safe and skip this paragraph if you feel reading about self-injury may trigger you.

112

repeatedly snap it as hard as I could. Counting numbly to well over a hundred, I wouldn't stop snapping until my arm was covered in black-and-blue bruises.

*At times, it was a form of punishing myself, like penance for all the ways I'd screwed up with Brooke; all the ways I'd failed God, my family, my dreams, myself. Other times, it was the only

*Words I wrote on my arm to
abstain from cutting*

*Trigger Warning:** Please keep yourself safe and skip this paragraph if you feel reading about self-injury may trigger you.

way I knew to feel or express my pain—a visible sign of my inward turmoil. I delayed cutting for as long as I could, trying to save it as a last resort. But there were days where all I could think about about was cutting, even as I fought to keep myself from doing it. Sometimes I took a pen or marker and wrote my emotions on my arm instead, as a way to express my feelings without doing actual harm. But in the end, the knife almost always won out because the physical pain on my body was still easier than the emotional pain in my soul. Often the bruises and scars from cutting would last for weeks or even months. Hiding them from others by wearing hoodies and pants, I found an odd sense of comfort when seeing them myself at home. It was proof that my pain was real. If no one else would validate me, then I would validate myself. But just like the secret my parents told me to hide forever, I hid my scars as well. They affirmed my buried pain and were the only evidence of what went on inside me.

· · · · ·

The fact that I relapsed though, was devastating to me. On top of all my other failures, it felt like the ultimate defeat. It was as if this one mistake with Brooke negated all that God called me to and permanently disqualified me from ministry. I was insufficient, dispensable, and quite sure God would never use me again. Maybe I should have never taken on this mission in the first place. I had failed in every way possible: I'd slept with the girl God wanted me to help, I'd broken my vow of purity, I'd committed the unforgiveable sin of homosexuality, *and* I'd relapsed into cutting, which was the very thing I was starting a ministry to help girls escape. I felt like a complete wreck and a total failure.

Life was looking pretty bleak. At that point, I still hoped to marry a man. I relied on my Christian principles and Focus upbringing to guide me through this mess I was in, and into my dreams for the future. The fact that my first love and first sexual experience were with a woman didn't convince me I was gay just yet. Instead, I did the same thing as my parents: chalked it all up to a big mistake that never should have happened, and worked to move forward from here. It wasn't enough yet to shatter my belief system, but it did definitely put a hole in it—a hole that, in time, led me on a journey of discovering who I truly am. But at that point, I was still holding onto my beliefs of what I'd been taught was right. And I was held captive by a secret that, at least for the time being, I told to no one.

As far as I knew, the only people that knew about what had happened between Brooke and me other than the two of us were Pastor Nadia, a few people that Brooke trusted, and my parents. The circle that held our secret was still quite small. But soon, paranoia crept in. I was sure if any of my peers knew, they would never want to spend time with me again. I was teaching piano lessons at the time, and I was certain that if the parents of my students knew, they would never leave their child alone with me again. I was convinced if people at church knew, they'd never let me serve in ministry again.

Even though none of these other people actually knew, I knew. And I couldn't stop wondering how everyone would treat me if they found out the truth of who I really was and what I'd done.

During those ten months of suffering in silence, Brooke called me occasionally, even though her pastor told her not to. Sometimes she would break all contact, only to reach out to me again out of a desire for love and connection. It was an exhausting, terrible cycle that became more vicious with each round.

Eventually, I had to cut ties with Brooke for good. I still longed to be a source of support to her as promised. I wanted to be her ally and listening ear in times of need. But, I could no longer offer her that.

I felt the way I imagine Lena may have felt when she walked out on me. Even though the situations were very different, my experience with Brooke helped me understand Lena a little more. But I didn't like feeling that way. I wanted to be better than Lena, tougher than Lena, stronger than Lena. But I had to come to terms with the fact that I couldn't save Brooke. Nothing I could do would stop her negative thought patterns, or convince her she was loved. I had to set her free to live her own life, so that I could be free myself.

Freedom. That's what I wanted. I had felt shackled by pain and failure and disappointment and silence for so long. I wanted to be free. My heart was suffocating and gasping for air. Now, with my relationship with Brooke finally behind me, after ten months of denying myself the basic human right of tears, I finally broke down and cried. I couldn't bear the weight of it any longer.

Curled up on the floor in the back corner of church one night and finally letting down my guard, I cried and cried and cried. For some time I had been afraid of releasing my pain. I wasn't sure I could handle the strong force of emotions that would come running out of a dam that had been so well built to protect my heart. Yet I was desperate to feel again—something, anything other than agony and disgrace. I was so ashamed: ashamed to approach my family, ashamed to approach God, ashamed to even look at myself. I longed to be free: freedom from guilt, freedom from shame, freedom from keeping secrets. Now that the nightmare with Brooke was finally over, I could start taking care of myself. The time had come to start my own journey of healing and freedom.

10

WRESTLING
WITH GOD

Recently, I was interviewed by a Christian therapist as a guest on her podcast. During our conversation, the topic of shame came up. With thirteen years of study on the topic of shame, author and speaker Dr. Brené Brown defines shame this way: *"Shame is the intensely painful feeling or experience of believing we are flawed and therefore unworthy of acceptance and belonging."*[5]

With that definition in mind, this therapist and I dissected the complexity that shame brings to our lives. She then asked how I felt shame had affected my own personal journey. I paused for a moment of reflection, and as I began to speak, I found myself surprised at my own answer. I suddenly realized that shame had been the root cause of almost every negative thing I've struggled with in my life:

---

5. Brené Brown, *Daring Greatly: How the Courage to Be Vulnerable Transforms the Way We Live, Love, Parent, and Lead* (New York: Avery, 2015).

I felt shame when I thought about my hair-pulling disorder and how self-conscious it made me feel about my appearance.

I felt shame when thinking about being depressed or having anxiety, and needing to go to counseling. The idea of not measuring up, despite my best efforts, weighed me down with shame.

I felt shame about the fact that I self-harmed. It was proof that I couldn't hold everything together. Even more shame washed over me when I relapsed after five years clean and after I already announced to everyone that I was starting a ministry to help girls who self-injured.

I felt shame for embarrassing my family by my sinful behavior with Brooke. Losing my purity, especially in *that* way, definitely did not uphold the family name in the way they expected of me.

I've become increasingly aware since that interview that shame has played a much bigger role in my life than I would like to admit. So much of my shame stems from the church. The judgment of people acting in the name of God is what so often planted my seeds of shame.

I remember the first time I saw Brooke laid out on the bed fully naked. She was so beautiful, it took my breath away. I know the first time she saw me unclothed, she thought the same. We were so in love. But because our families and our churches told us it was wrong to love another woman, our love was stained by shame. I often wonder what our relationship would have looked like if neither of us had been taught that homosexuality was wrong and sinful. I don't think it would have been a lasting relationship—we both carried too much baggage at that time—but we would have been free of all the needless turmoil and agony brought on by shame.

After cutting ties with Brooke, I began an inner pilgrimage to find freedom from shame. I was sick of cheap imitations of the voice of God handed to me by others and needed to rekindle my own relationship with the Father/Mother of my heart.

What I didn't realize at the time, was that while those ten post-Brooke months of silence I endured may have protected my reputation from the judgment of others, they also isolated me from the love of God. Steeped in shame, I didn't believe I deserved to approach my Maker. Instead, I believed a lie that my love for Brooke made me exempt from the forgiveness, mercy, and love of God.

On one of the Sundays that I actually did make it to church, despite my anxiety of being found out and judged a hypocrite, I had a realization. During worship, which is when I always seem to hear God the clearest, I dared to approach God once again. I was more timid than before and second-guessed my right to be there. But I did my best to silence all the condemning voices buzzing around in my head. In the stillness of the moment I began to recognize that for me to believe I was excluded from the love of God also meant that I believed the death of Jesus was in vain—that the blood he shed on the cross was enough for everyone else, but not enough for me. It convicted me, and I intentionally redirected my heart back to truth: Jesus was indeed enough, even for me.

But I still struggled. I felt frail, alone, and vulnerable. My raw humanity felt at odds with a God whose love seemed conditional. My church and family taught me that God loves you if you're good, but if you make a mistake (especially a mistake as bad as homosexuality) then you are bad, and God is mad at you and abhors your behavior. It may not have been explicitly stated that way, but the implication was clear.

It was clear from the pulpit when youth pastors emphasized the importance of spending at least one hour in prayer and Bible study every day and fasting on a regular basis. Anything less was sub-par. It was clear from the Focus on the Family teachings that you fight against the temptations of your earthly body in order to please a heavenly God. Failure to do this was weakness and lack of faith and perseverance. It was clear in the faces of my parents when they heard about my relationship with Brooke. They were angry with me. God was angry with me. I hadn't measured up.

This wasn't the God I knew in my teen years. The moments we spent together were so sweet and precious. Now, I felt split between what I knew of God personally and what prominent Christian leaders had taught me about God. That confusion launched me into my own journey of exploration. I began to wrestle with God and the questions that bombarded my heart.

Up until that point in my life, I largely thought the way I was conditioned to think. My parents embraced and implemented the Focus on the Family ideal that taught you to encase your children in a Christian environment in order to protect them from the outside world. I know they had great intentions, but in hindsight, being swaddled in a Christian bubble hindered my ability to function in the real world.

From a young age, I was not given an opportunity to think for myself. I was told what to think and how I should feel in almost every situation. As a result, I couldn't really defend what I believed, because everyone around me believed exactly the same way I did. Without exposure to diversity (people of color, people with disabilities, with different sexual orientations, gender identities, and belief systems) I wasn't able to appreciate and respect all the different shapes and forms that God comes in. That knowledge would have helped me appreciate the world at large and become a more well-rounded individual.

Instead, I was taught to love everyone, but with the condition that we love them in order to make them like us: good Christians who love God and do what the Bible commands. If they weren't Christians, then the goal was to convince them to want to become one. If they were Christians, then the goal was to "be a blessing to them" just as my mom trained us to do. I did many great things in order to bless and serve others—I sang and performed all over the world, I went on mission trips, I reached out to people who were struggling—but looking back, I wish I had done more of it without strings attached. Yet that was all I knew to do. I had been molded into a Christian cliché. But now, the mold was getting uncomfortable.

At the age of twenty-six, I finally started to break out of that mold. It was long overdue. Though intimidating at first, I finally began thinking for myself, instead of through the lens of my parents' worldview. It was the first time I'd begun to wonder what the world looked like outside this box I lived in. In this place of wondering, I started asking questions:

Am I deceived to believe that I did the right thing in taking Brooke into my home?
Is what everyone said about Brooke and me true and I'm the one believing the lie?
Is my soul now damned to hell for what happened between us?
Did I really even hear God in the first place?

I was so sure when I first met Brooke that God was calling me to minister to her. But now, several months after she left, I doubted. I wondered where I went wrong along the way.

Then I started asking other questions:

Why have I never had a boyfriend?
Why have I never been asked out on a date?
Why have I never been kissed?
Is there something wrong with me?

I decided two things were necessary: counseling and dating. I figured the answer to these confusing and heart-wrenching questions might lie in the fact that I had never been on a date with anyone . . . ever! And if the answers didn't lie in dating, then surely they would lie inside a therapist's office. So I decided to start dating and see what revelations came my way, and I also enrolled in therapy.

Morgan was my new therapist, and she let me bring all parts of myself to the table: my faith, my family, my sexuality, my questions; there weren't any limitations when I came to her office. She even let me bring my Shih-Tzu/Maltese puppy, Half Pint, because she knew it was helpful and calming for me. Morgan was the first person to give me permission to explore who I was. No one had done that for me before. Each week I came with my heavy heart and we unpacked a little more. I told her my fear of going to hell. I explained to her the Christian belief that being gay put my soul in jeopardy. I opened up and told her that every time something went wrong in my life—a bad day, a flat tire, an unexpected death—I felt it was God's punishment for the feelings I harbored inside. I wanted to get rid of them. I wanted to be normal. But no matter how hard I tried, the feelings wouldn't go away. My anxiety rose higher and higher as I feared what would happen to me if I got in a fatal car crash or went to bed one night and simply didn't wake up. Would my soul be damned to an eternity in hell because I hadn't been able to resolve or pray away my gay feelings? Would I be separated from my family and friends and all those I love forever because there was a part of me that I didn't ask for, yet couldn't get rid of? I just wanted to be like everyone else. I wanted to belong. I felt so isolated and alone in my fear.

Week after week, Morgan helped me process my fears as we sorted through my emotions around Brooke, around my parents, around my faith, around life after death, and around sexuality. She gave me permission to be free from the pressure of labeling myself as gay or straight.

· · · · ·

One day I walked into counseling to find Morgan sitting there with a basket of rocks and a marker. She explained that on each rock, she wanted me to write a feeling, a struggle, or the name of a person. Then, when I was through, I would tell her what each represented and why I'd chosen it. It was meant to be a tangible representation of my inward struggles.

I sat for a moment, pondering the name of my rocks. Then, getting up from the couch and sitting on the floor, I dumped them all in a pile. On the first rock, I wrote **Me** and placed it in the middle of the floor. On another rock, I wrote **Lesbian???/Scared of Hell** and set it down. On the next I wrote **Shame**, and then set it aside. After getting started, I was on a roll and continued with rocks labeled **Mom/Dad**, **Daniel**, and **God**. Then I went on labeling others things like **PTSD**, **Stuffed**

Emotions, Hair-Pulling, Self-Harm, and on it went. I came up with so many labels that I ran out of rocks, and Morgan had to go to the parking lot to collect more.

I don't think this was part of the assignment, but I then started arranging my rocks on the carpet like a puzzle. With the rock representing **Me** at the center, I placed each of the other rocks around it in relation to where I felt they were in my life. Morgan sat patiently as I worked in silence for a good ten minutes. When I finished, I sat back and looked at her. She nodded and said, "Okay. Tell me about your rocks."

I explained to her this newfound map of my life, telling her where I placed everything and why. I told her I placed the **PTSD** rock together with the ones labeled **Stuffed Emotions** and **Hair-Pulling** because they seemed to come hand-in-hand, though they didn't surface every day. They were stationed in the top left corner of my life picture. I placed the **Mom/Dad** rock as well as the one for my brother **Daniel** far away in the top right corner with another one labeled **Outcast/Leper/Misfit** directly on top of them, indicating with the distance, that I was having to pull away from them more and more because **Outcast/Leper/Misfit** is how being around them made me feel. I placed **God** fairly close to **Me** but just a little apart because I wasn't sure how all these struggles made me feel about God, or how God felt about me. Afraid that the possibility of being gay would rob me of my salvation, I was confused about the love versus judgment of God.

The more I explained this visual representation of my emotions to my counselor, the more therapeutic it became. It helped me make sense of my life and gave me the opportunity to look at it in an organized fashion, manipulating the location of the different pieces based on how I felt about each. It gave me a sense of control when so many things in my life felt so out of control.

It also gave me the chance to identify my emotions. The insulated environment I grew up in kept me from exploring feelings the way I should have. I often struggled to express myself and had difficulty labeling what I was feeling when emotions other than happy surfaced. They felt like a jumbled mess inside. At least with my rocks, my feelings had a name. Labeling them helped me understand them, which in turn, helped me better understand my life as a whole.

Envisioning my map of rocks helped me start to make sense of the war raging inside me. I felt divided. It was as if half of me belonged in one world and half of me belonged in another, and it seemed impossible that these two worlds would ever meld into one. I was facing an ultimatum between my faith in God and my sexuality. I was unable to deny my love for Jesus, but equally unable to make my love and attraction toward women disappear. No matter how hard I prayed or how many good things I did or how hard I tried to like boys, this disjointed feeling wouldn't go away. It tore my heart in two. Fasting and praying, I begged God to take these feelings away from me, to heal me, to make me normal; I promised anything in return. I loved Jesus! I didn't want to go to hell! I didn't want to be separated from my family or lose my friends.

"Haven't I been through enough?" I'd shout at God. "Why this? Why *me*?"

The complexity of this war inside overwhelmed me—I can only describe it as torture. I reached a point where I realized that if I didn't face this and find a way to make peace with

My basket of rocks

Rocks used in therapy prior to coming out

it, I was going to die. I'd had almost four years of feeling at odds within myself and I was now at the point where I knew I couldn't survive it much longer. Thoughts of suicide began to haunt me. I didn't know where or how. I just knew how isolated I felt in my struggle. The scrutinizing eyes and whispers behind my back from friends and family told me I was unlovable. It taught me to be ashamed of who I was. I knew I had to find answers. If I wanted to survive, I had to fight for my life. Part of sorting through those emotions came by working with my basket of rocks.

Morgan held on to my basket of rocks for me from week to week, and occasionally we pulled them out and reassessed how things were going. I moved the rocks closer or farther apart from previous meetings based on how my life was progressing. Over time, if I settled a certain issue, that rock was thrown away. But likewise, as we went on, new rocks like **Coming Out, Fear of Rejection**, and **Desire for Girlfriend?** were added.

Of all the counselors I've seen over the years, Morgan was the most helpful, and this was the single most effective exercise I've ever done. I still have some of my rocks to this day, and on occasion, still dump them out and organize them on the floor to assess myself. It continues to be therapeutic for me.

• • • • •

While working through things in counseling, I also worked on the second half of the puzzle and reluctantly went on some dates with men. Knowing this was the fairy tale I was supposed to want, I tried my best to go with an open mind and have a good time. But in reality, I never enjoyed it much. It's not that I'm repulsed by men (though some of them were quite repulsive);

I just didn't feel anything—no connection, no spark, no butterflies. I enjoyed the attention, but felt edgy, awkward, and uncomfortable around them, not excited.

There was one exception to this: his name was Darius. If I ever had a chance at a successful straight relationship, Darius was it. We got to know one another and there was a connection . . . of sorts. I certainly enjoyed being with Darius more than any of the other guys I went out with. Haunted by the straight person's myth that you "just haven't met the right guy yet," or the skeptic's theory that "you just don't like guys because you've never been with one," I decided that if I was going to end up being gay, it wouldn't be for lack of trying to be straight. So I gave it my all.

One huge surprise I had as I began to date men was that my virginity (or, at least, the fact that I had never had sex with a man) wasn't valued by these men the way I expected it to be. Contrary to what I was taught, the men I met were actually intimidated by my lack of experience, including Darius. It caused me to feel embarrassed by my virginity, rather than proud of it. Another disservice done to me by the purity culture, I was ill prepared for life outside my Christian community.

But ultimately, the pressure to fit in to society's norms still led me to have sex with Darius. I felt obligated to do it because of my Christianity, in a weird sort of way. On one hand, sex outside of marriage was a sin highly frowned upon. On the other hand, if I was gay, I felt I owed it to my faith somehow to prove that I'd given being straight my best attempt.

Sleeping with Darius turned out to be very eye-opening for me. This was the moment I'd waited for all my life. Though we certainly didn't "save sex for marriage" as Christianity taught, I still expected this moment to somehow launch me into sexual bliss as a reward for all the years I'd saved myself and waited. Maybe deep down, I did expect it to make me straight. But that's not what happened. Instead, I was disappointed. There was no real excitement over the fact that I'd just had sex with a man for the first time. Instead, I felt cheated. I found myself thinking, "I've waited all my life for *this*???" It was completely unsatisfying. I know that for most people (especially straight women) the first time isn't the best, but the emotional connection between Darius and me wasn't anything like the emotional connection I felt with Brooke. Being with Brooke was natural and easy. Being with Darius was awkward and forced. I left that night feeling deceived by Christians and the purity culture I'd been a part of.

In the days following, I found that I hardly gave that night with Darius a second thought. It felt meaningless to me. So I stepped outside the lines a little more and dated a few women. It was a risk that I spoke of to no one, yet felt I had to take. After several dates with one woman, we kissed. Then I realized something. I found myself obsessing way more over this girl I'd simply kissed than I thought about the entire sexual experience I'd shared with Darius.

That's when the light bulb lit up: there was a significant difference for me in the connection I felt with each sex. I'd known Darius longer than the woman I dated, but when I thought about my simple kiss with her, it made my head spin and sent butterflies to my stomach. When I thought about my time with Darius, I felt nothing. Deep inside I knew then that I was gay. But I still wasn't ready to admit it, even to myself, because I still didn't know what being gay would mean for my relationship with God.

• • • • •

I was on my way out of the grocery store one afternoon when I stopped by Redbox to see what new movies were out. Scrolling through the titles on the screen, I saw one I hadn't heard of before. It was called *Prayers for Bobby*. Starring Sigourney Weaver, it caught my attention and I clicked on the title for more information. Reading the film description, I saw two words I'd never seen put side by side before: *gay* and *Christian*. My eyes widened. You mean, this is a thing? I'm not the only one that feels like a social and religious outcast? Eager to know more about this, I swiped my card to pay for the film and took it home.

In the privacy of my bedroom that night, I watched the true story of a boy named Bobby Griffith. He was the perfect son, the favorite child, until Bobby realized he was gay and came out to his family. This caused Bobby's mother, Mary, to turn to her conservative and fundamentalist beliefs in an attempt to rescue Bobby from what she felt was the unforgiveable sin.

During the first half of the movie, so much of it paralleled my own life that it was painful. This was *my* life I was watching. The way Bobbie confided only in his journals was just like me. The anxiety he confessed over going to hell was the same anxiety I felt. The fear over losing his family, his friends, and all he held dear was the very fear I was facing. The way his prayers never seemed to be enough to rid him of his gayness, the pressure he felt to conform to his family's desires, the way he was told he wasn't being healed because he didn't have enough faith and wasn't trying hard enough—all of this mirrored *my* very deep and painful experiences. My eyes were glued to the screen.

Once Bobby's mom realized that her efforts at saving Bobby weren't producing any change, she did the very thing Bobby feared: she rejected him. The pain and exclusion Bobby felt was too much for him to bear. Overcome by the war raging inside him, Bobby jumped from a bridge to his death.

Now I was sobbing. I related to that paralyzing fear of being rejected by those you love the most. I feared that Bobby's fate would be my own. I knew this at-the-end-of-your-rope feeling. I knew the isolation and intense loneliness of wrestling with the unspeakable. I knew the overwhelming seas of emotion.

After Bobby's death, Mary wrestled for a place to pin the blame. Out of desperation and struggle, she reached out to an affirming pastor in the gay community and eventually saw the love of God for all the diversity it really holds. In the dim light of a chapel on a rainy night, Mary broke down in tears as she came to the realization that her own ignorance and lack of acceptance is what really killed her son.

I cried for Mary. I cried for Bobby. I cried for me. The story of the Griffith family foretold my story as I saw it unfolding in the months to come. It magnified my hidden fears and put them right before my eyes. I trembled inside at the thought that my life was about to unravel.

At this point, things in my life were still somewhat intact. I had cleaned up the outward pieces from the mess with Brooke and escaped with only my parents knowing about it. My parents and I still spent time together frequently, and the awkward moments between us around what had happened with Brooke were minimal. They were just as good at compartmentalizing as I was. Though they did start analyzing my friends a lot more closely, they didn't mention Brooke very often. Instead, they chose to see the whole situation as a big mistake. Like everything else, they wanted to just sweep it under the rug, forget about it, and move on with our Focus on the Family façade.

That was fine with me. I knew from my parents' reaction to what had already happened when they heard about Brooke, that involving them in my exploration of sexuality and faith wasn't an option. So I played their game to please them, while searching for truth on my own. They had already silenced me once. I wasn't going to let it happen again.

· · · · ·

Watching *Prayers for Bobby* was the first time that I realized I was not alone in my struggle. Up until then, I thought that I was the only one in the world who was misfit enough to turn up gay in a conservative, fundamentalist, Christian family. But after seeing the movie, I saw that there was at least one other person like me. And if there was one, perhaps there were two, or three, or possibly more.

This epiphany led me to start researching who else might be out there like me. Previously, I thought that any organization or group of people that claimed to be both gay and Christian was a farce. It was impossible to be both. They were two opposing worlds that did *not* intersect. But now curiosity piqued my interest and I decided to risk looking outside my box a little further.

In order to do that, I needed to put some distance between me and the judgmental people in my life. I knew I couldn't hear the fresh voice of God if all that played in my head were negative tapes that God hated me. So I did my best to keep those voices at a distance. This even included walking away from church for a time. I let very few people in on my actual process, and with a clean slate, I began a new phase of my journey. Looking back, I now realize there was real wisdom in this. Distancing myself from those negative voices and letting God alone define me was indeed the very key to finding what set me free.

I was about to undertake what felt like an enormous endeavor: to search for others who, like me, felt like they were both gay and Christian, and also to finally look at what the Bible really said about homosexuality. I was terrified. I didn't want to water down the gospel just to make myself comfortable, nor did I want to miss a hidden truth of God just because I was comfortable in a box or listened to the wrong people. I was terrified to find out that God *did* approve of same-sex relationships and I was equally terrified to find out that God *did not* approve of them. I knew either way, my life was about to drastically change. Taking a deep breath, I sat down at my computer and opened my web browser, ready to start my quest for truth.

11

LET US LIVE
AND LOVE
WITHOUT LABELS

I was raised to believe that there is one kind of family. In the evangelical Christian world, the proper family is a married couple (one man and one woman) who together raise children under the guidance of Christ. Bonus points are given to those who adopt, for they are doing the honorable work of God by caring for innocent children who've been mistreated or victimized. Anything other than that family formula is unacceptable. Those who get pregnant before they are married, or those who live with their boyfriend or girlfriend without being married, or those who have an abortion, are all outside the will of God and the design he established for marriage and the family institution.

Being gay is so far outside of those parameters it doesn't even fit into the outer realms of unacceptable families. It's just off the radar completely. Homosexual thoughts are considered dirty and disgusting, not to mention sinful. Gay families are thought of as a joke—a perfect example of just how far humanity has fallen from God's intended plan.

Even as the rest of Western culture has evolved to accept gay relationships, evangelical Christians have not. I was shocked at some of the comments I heard in a recent episode of Dr. Dobson's *Family Talk* podcast that featured a conversation with Franklin Graham. "We have allowed the enemy to come into our churches," said Graham. "I was talking to some Christians [who] invited these gay children to come into their home and to come to church, [because they wanted] to influence them. And I thought to myself, those parents aren't going to influence those kids; those kids are going to influence those parents' children. We have to understand who the enemy is and what he wants to do. He wants to devour our homes. He wants to devour this nation. We have to be so careful who we let our kids hang out with. We have to be so careful who we let into the churches. We have immoral people that get into our churches and it begins to affect the others in the church and it is dangerous. You cannot stay gay and call yourself a Christian."[6]

Dobson then followed this comment with a horribly faulty and inaccurate definition of bisexuality: "You know what the 'B' [in LGBTQ] stands for? Bisexual. That's orgies! That's lots of sex with lots of people."

These erroneous comments shape the beliefs of evangelical Christians around the globe and provide a grossly misguided view of the LGBTQ community. Mel White, executive director of SoulForce, along with many others tried to warn Dobson of his harmful teachings when they protested Dobson's campaign

---

6. http://tinyurl.com/drjamesdobson

against same-sex rights and gay marriage at Focus on the Family in 2005.

"We are here to say, Jim, we love you enough to stop you from doing the damage you are doing to families across the nation," Mel White said.[7]

If Dobson had taken to heart the message Mel White and others were communicating instead of brushing it aside as warped theology, he could have stopped these misguided beliefs and faulty teachings from affecting his 220 million followers worldwide. If he had listened, lives could have been saved, rather than lost to suicide. If he had listened, families could have been strengthened and restored, rather than torn apart—perhaps my family could have been one of them. But instead, Focus on the Family continues to have a political agenda and Dobson's teachings continue to harm countless gay Christians and their families, driving many away from the church and from God.

The real truth—the truth I've come to know through the extensive research that lies outside of Dr. Dobson and Franklin Graham's teachings—is that God's love comes in many more forms than what Dobson, Graham, or many other evangelicals allow space for.

I can say that with confidence now. But with my limited knowledge and worldview growing up, I was still under the influence of these types of beliefs, and therefore also unaware of all the beautiful diversity among humankind that God created. Something inside me told me there was more, but I had yet to find it.

---

7. http://trib.com/news/state-and-regional/gay-rights-supporters-protest-outside -focus/article_69f9cdbe-0100-5e5d-928e-f7c9611b55df.html.

Sitting down at my computer, beginning my quest for truth about how God really feels about people with same-sex attractions, I typed "Gay Christian Churches in Colorado" into my web browser. I forced a deep breath, allowing space to feel both fear and hope as the search engine combed the web for results.

Because Colorado Springs is a conservative, military town and the headquarters for numerous Christian ministries, I wasn't surprised that I didn't find any gay-affirming churches in my immediate area. But I kept searching, knowing that if I was going to find a gay-affirming home church, it had to have a strong biblical basis. I didn't want a group of people who condoned homosexuality merely for the sake of comfort and acceptance, nor did I want to find a way to simply justify my way of life. I wanted the truth. I wanted something that was biblically sound, but also allowed people to come as they are—if that even existed.

The only church on the list that even looked like a remote possibility was a place called Highlands Church in north Denver. Curious and desperate for a lifeline—anything that might offer me some hope—I clicked on the link that rerouted me to their website. The first thing I saw on their home page when it loaded was their ethos. It read,

Married, divorced, and single here,
it's one family that mingles here.
Conservative and liberal here, we've all gotta give a little here.
Big and small here, there's room for us all here.
Doubt and believe here, we all can receive here.
LGBTQ and straight here, there's no hate here.
Woman and man here, everyone can here.
Whatever your race here, for all of us grace here.

In imitation of the ridiculous love that almighty God has for each of us and all of us, we choose to **Live and Love without Labels**.[8]

Tears welled in my eyes. Could this be real? Did a place for people like me, who were attracted to the same sex but really loved God, actually exist? I decided to email the pastor and find out. Unsure whether I was writing out of hope or sheer desperation (or perhaps both), I poured out my broken heart to this pastor whom I'd never met. I told him about Brooke, I told him about my family, I told him about my shame, and I asked for help. Then, with trepidation, I hit "Send."

I didn't have to wait long for a reply. Hardly three hours went by before I received a very long, heartfelt response from the founding pastor, Mark Tidd. Although he's straight, he empathized with my struggle. With the compassion of a father, he expressed deep love for and acceptance of me. He spoke the words I was longing to hear but struggled to believe: God loves me exactly the way that I am and I don't have to change anything to be accepted by him. He extended an invitation to visit Highlands Church and said if I was interested, he would contact a couple of girls to show me around and take me to lunch after the service. It seemed too good to be true. But knowing the critical place I was in, I took the risk and said yes.

Driving to Denver that following Sunday, my heart raced at highway speed as my hands gripped the steering wheel tighter and tighter. I didn't know what to expect. I was afraid to get my

---

8. Written by and used with the blessing of Mark Tidd, Highlands Church Denver.

hopes up, only to be disappointed. But I desperately needed this to be the answer I'd been searching for. Feeling unwelcome at church ever since the last time I trusted a pastor with my secret, it was vital to my soul that this experience be different. My life was hanging in the balance.

I nervously parked in a small parking lot on the corner of 32nd and Lowell Blvd and took a moment to breathe. The pastor had indeed given me the contacts of two girls to meet up with. Were they friends? Were they a couple? I had no idea. Other than the girl I dated for a short time after Darius, I'd never met another openly gay person before. This was new ground for me.

Part of me wondered how I would measure up against what I saw. I tend to be a feminine girl, and I wondered if it was even possible for a girl like me to be gay. Or would I have to change my appearance (cut my hair or wear more masculine clothes for example) to fit in? The answer to so many of my questions lay just inside those church doors on the other side of the parking lot.

The two girls, who indeed were a couple, were there waiting for me when I arrived. They looked unusually normal. In fact, as I looked around, I noticed that everyone inside looked normal. Women of all hair lengths and styles mingled about—some in skirts or dresses, others in jeans and T-shirts. The men looked equally ordinary. Suit jackets, polo shirts, and jeans were mix-matched with clean-cut and scruffy hairstyles.

There were no rainbow flags or drag queens; there weren't any protestors at the door with "God Hates Fags" signs or people making out in the lobby. What I saw was not what I was taught to expect at a gathering that welcomed gay people. Instead, these casual, normal-looking people were gathering together, hugging and greeting one another like you would expect to see

Visiting Highlands Church for the first time

at any church. I took mental notes on everything and adjusted my expectations accordingly as I stood in the lobby. I immediately experienced an overwhelming sense of authenticity, acceptance, and love. Perfect strangers warmly embraced me and welcomed me as though they'd known me all their lives. They seemed genuinely happy to meet me and have me there.

One tall, husky man heard it was my first time and that my dad worked at Focus. He didn't even speak a word. He just moved in and gave me a big bear hug, as if to say, "I can only imagine how much you must be going through." I almost broke down in tears right there.

As the service started, I took my seat, and began to take in the experience. After several songs, Pastor Mark took the stage. The first words out of his mouth were those of the ethos I saw online. Hearing these words said aloud in this space made me feel safe in a church for the first time in almost five years. My heart began to melt, hanging on his every word.

". . . In imitation of the ridiculous love that almighty God has for each of us and all of us, we choose to live and love without labels. Amen?"

"Amen!" the congregation answered back.

Without labels. I thought about that phrase for a moment, trying to wrap my mind around what that meant. I'd felt tied to labels for as long as I could remember. Was this man, this *pastor*, really releasing me from the weight of appearances I'd felt pressured to uphold my entire life? I'd always felt the need for labels. These descriptors explained to others who I was. I was a *Christian*, I was *Home-schooled*, I was a *Daughter of a Focus on the Family executive*, I was *Daniel's sister*, I was the *Green Gable Girls leader's daughter*, I was a *musician*. I was supposed to be *happy*, *blessed*, a *role model* for others. Labels defined me. Labels of shame, labels of perfection, labels of destruction. Some labels I still wrestled with. Was I gay or straight? Was I still a Christian, or did this act now thrust me outside the realm of God's acceptance? Could I be both gay *and* Christian? So much depended on labels, on appearances, on acceptance. Was there really such a place where I could come and be free of all of these defining words that stuck to me and bogged me down?

As I listened to Pastor Mark speak these words of acceptance and life, my feelings of isolation softened a bit. I could feel the Holy Spirit whispering to me that this was the safe place I'd been searching for. I had finally found other people like me and a sanctuary for my heart to rest.

These people gathered together in a place where they could bring all of who they were and sit under the teachings of pastors who believed and taught the Bible from an evangelical point of view. Yet, in the midst of their sound biblical theology, they weren't afraid to question or doubt or explore beliefs outside the normal boundaries that Christians tend to live within. They didn't feel threatened by new ideas or different interpretations of the Scriptures the way so many other Christians I'd met seemed to be. But at the same time, they weren't throwing the Bible out or molding it to read the way they wanted it to just to make them comfortable either. It was a beautiful balance, and a freeing one. It was authentic, it was real, and my heart finally felt at home.

That day, January 8, 2012, was a turning point for me. I went home and wrote in my journal for the first time in three years, because it was the first time I'd felt hope in three years. From then on, I didn't know what the future held, but I knew Highlands Church had to be a part of it.

I drove to Denver every Sunday that I could manage in the following weeks, trying to go to lunch with somebody new after every Highlands service. As I got to know these people, I was amazed at how genuine and real they were. I saw couples who talked about their love for their same-sex partner or spouse and their love for God in the same context without any conflict in between. It was the most beautiful thing I'd ever seen. Some of the couples I met had been together for ten, fifteen, even twenty-five years. Seeing their love for God and their love for each other normalized these two seemingly opposing worlds and married them in a way that I'd previously been unable to join together. It was what my heart ached for—to know it was possible to both love God and a person of the same gender. I was seeing it with my own eyes and it was captivating. In spite of their struggle to get where they were, or perhaps because of it, they were the most humble, authentic, genuine group of people I'd ever met. Seeing that it was possible gave me the courage to turn the corner and start accepting myself for who I was.

Although I was well on my way, before I could fully embrace myself, I still needed to examine on my own what the Bible really said about homosexuality. I asked around and was given the name of a few books. Unfortunately, books like *Torn* by Justin Lee and *God and the Gay Christian* by Matthew Vines weren't available yet. I consider those, along with Kathy Baldock's *Walking the Bridgeless Canyon* and Susan Cottrell's *"Mom, I'm Gay"—Loving Your LGBTQ Child and Strengthening Your Faith* to be among the best resources currently on the market for gay Christians and their families/friends today. But at the time I was getting ready to come out, the LGBTQ Christian movement hadn't quite picked up enough steam to really get off the ground. So instead, I read a book by Daniel A. Helminiak titled *What the Bible Really Says About Homosexuality*. Though somewhat heavy and dense with information, it walked me through each of the Scriptures known as the "clobber passages" (the Bible verses that are believed by many to reference homosexuality). With an unbiased approach, Helminiak gave a historical and cultural background to the verses, placing them in the context of the times in which they were written. It provided me with the knowledge I needed to wrap my brain around what my heart was already finding to be true. Along with books like *It Gets Better* by Dan Savage and Terry Miller, which provided stories of other LGBTQ people from all walks of life, it helped me find peace. My head and my heart began to unite.

• • • • •

The knowledge I'd gained through reading and research, combined with the way I was experiencing God with other gay Christians and straight allies at Highlands, made me realize I had a decision to make: I could wither away in a life of fear and shame and condemnation, or I could live a life of truly trusting God. The kind of trust that was required of me to truly accept myself was a depth of trust in God I'd never known before.

It became clear that no amount of works or good deeds or prayer was going to make me straight. I was gay. So all I could do was trust that God knew what he was doing the day he created me, and that I wasn't a mistake. For the first time I realized how completely dependent I was on the grace and mercy of God. Being gay was out of my control, just like where I would spend eternity was out of my control. I couldn't earn my way to heaven any more than I could earn my way out of being gay.

I looked toward a future that was totally contradictory to what I'd been taught my entire life. With two completely opposing views of Scripture on homosexuality, how was I ever to know for sure which is truly right? How was I ever to know for sure if my soul was truly safe in eternity?

For me, it came down to the simple yet difficult act of trust. I had to make a conscious decision to trust in the mercy and goodness of who I knew God to be and live in that grace every day.

Many people believe the myth that people choose to be gay. I can guarantee you that given the chance, no one in their right mind would ever choose to be gay. But what I do choose is to believe that God is who he says he is. I choose to trust in a God who is good, and loving, and kind. And I choose to lean on his grace and mercy every single day.

Coming to terms with this need for trust and dependence on God's grace is what finally set my soul at rest. Feelings of doubt were lifted, and I experienced a deep inner peace. My relationship with God became more authentic and more genuine than it had ever been. For the first time, my faith wasn't about impressing God, or pleasing God, or putting on a good show for him to earn his favor; it was based on the attitude of my heart. It was centered in grace rather than striving for perfection.

My heart had camped in the midst of angst, worry, fear, and doubt for so long. But eventually, I realized that these are not attributes of God. Jesus said, "Every good tree bears good fruit, but a bad tree bears bad fruit. A good tree cannot bear bad fruit, and a bad tree cannot bear good fruit. Therefore, by their fruits you shall know them" (Matthew 7:17–18, 20). The love I experienced when attending Highlands Church, the peace I began feeling deep inside about my sexuality, the joy I found in knowing I am beautifully unique—these were the fruits of the Spirit that told me I was in a good and healthy place.

With this newfound peace taking root in the center of my soul, I began settling into myself and even finding some joy. I recognized myself as part of the LGBTQ community, and slowly started self-identifying as gay. It was a new world for me, but one that felt right and good.

Once all the knowledge, experience, and peace I gained from trusting God fused together, a sort of domino effect occurred. All the answers to the questions I'd been wrestling with in silence for years suddenly started locking into place.

I remember the very first time I prayed to God for my spouse as a woman rather than as a man. Excitement bubbled in my spirit in the place that guilt and shame once resided. The conflict I had once felt inside was disintegrating.

While the newfound peace I felt inside my own skin was bringing moments of joy, I feared what was to come. I started confiding in a few friends and coming out to those I felt were the safest. My Wiccan neighbor was thrilled that I was finally breaking out of the confines of my religion. Stacy, my best friend from college, was supportive and behind me all the way. I even had a couple of people tell me that this didn't come as a surprise to them. They'd known and were just waiting for me to tell them. It baffled me that someone else could know I was gay before I even knew myself. But they did, and were just quietly waiting for me to come out to them.

When I had a few positive coming-out experiences behind me, I moved down the list of who I needed to tell next. I was playing my cards very strategically and made sure to not tell anyone who knew my parents before I was ready to tell my parents myself. I didn't want to put anyone in the awkward position of having to keep a secret, nor did I want my parents to hear it from someone else. I wanted to make sure they heard it from me first. I felt I owed them that much.

I did choose one friend of my mom's who I felt deserved to hear it from me, yet I knew would also be a great source of support for my mom once I'd come out to my family. Her name was Betsy. I didn't know how my parents would react when I told them, but I knew the time to tell them was coming, and that when it did, they were going to need support. So I told Betsy I had something important to tell her and asked if she would come to my house for a visit. She sat and listened graciously as I fumbled over my words, trying to get to the point of why I'd asked her to come. When I finally spit the news out that I was gay, she calmly asked a few questions:

When are you planning to tell your parents? Do they have any idea? How do you know that God is okay with this?

I struggled to explain the peace I'd found. It was a bumpy conversation, but Betsy was kind and loving, despite whatever personal feelings she had, and tried to console me with the fact that she loved me, my parents loved me, and everything was going to be okay.

I breathed a sigh of relief when the conversation was over. Betsy's family had been very close friends of our family for many years. I taught her daughter piano lessons; we shared in holidays and celebrations together. I was grateful that at least one of the more difficult people to tell was now done with, and that it seemed to go fairly well. I thought maybe things would turn out okay after all.

But two days later, the phone rang. It was Betsy. She asked if she could come back to my place again, saying she needed to talk to me. A nervous ball formed in the pit of my stomach as I wondered what this was about. I was unsure if she just had more questions, or if it was something more serious.

When she walked in the door of my apartment, I could see she was troubled. Torn between her love and concern for me as a friend, and her respect for her husband, she sadly told me that she was pulling her daughter from piano lessons with me. She admitted she didn't understand the struggle I was going through, but explained that her husband firmly believed it was a matter of spiritual warfare and that they could no longer allow their daughter to be under my influence.

Her daughter, who was a joy to teach, never showed up at my home for lessons again. Just as I feared, I was viewed as a spiritual deviant. Even worse, the labels so often assigned to gay people as perverts, child molesters, and pedophiles were now being applied to me. Labels were the very thing I was trying to break free of. Yet once again, they were being forced upon me. And these labels were the worst ones of all. They were more than devastating. They were dehumanizing.

This was my first glimpse into what my life was about to look like once I came out to everyone. This wasn't sunshine and rainbows. This wasn't a joke. This was heavy, and this was real. This was my life, and it was about to unravel.

I knew that I couldn't wait very long before telling my parents. Whatever the outcome, my family needed to know. Now that my heart and head were finally aligned under the peace of Christ, I couldn't keep it a secret any longer. I didn't want to live a double life and I refused to be a hypocrite. I was tired of having to filter everything I said around my family in order to keep them comfortable. I was sick of having to watch my words out of fear that they would find out before I was ready. Putting on a show was taxing on my brain and draining for my soul.

I decided that since I was finally at peace with myself, I couldn't deal with that pressure anymore. There was no reason to wait any longer. Whatever their reaction was going to be, I had to do this. I owed it to them to tell them the truth, and I owed it to myself to be free from living a lie. I could feel inside my spirit that the time to tell my parents I was gay was coming very soon.

12

RIDING THE
TIGHTROPE

The year before I came out to my family, I found a photograph
of a man who had strung a tightrope across Niagara Falls from
one side to the other. He frequently walked the tightrope back
and forth, pushing a wheelbarrow out in front of him as he
went. He asked an onlooker who stopped to watch, "Do you
think I can do it?"

"I know you can do it," replied the man. "I've seen you do it
a dozen times."

The tightrope walker responded, "Then get in the
wheelbarrow."

I kept that picture taped to my fridge for an entire year
before coming out to my family. It haunted me daily, posing the
question—do I trust God enough to metaphorically get in the
wheelbarrow and come out to my family?

Nothing was more terrifying.

In the weeks leading up to my coming out, I was both
excited to be free from the weight I'd silently carried and

Picture of the photo taped to my fridge before I came out

deeply anxious about how this would affect my relationship with my family. I didn't know what to expect or how they would react. I knew they wouldn't agree or be happy for me, but I didn't have a good gauge for how positive or negative their reaction would be. Anything from simply disagreeing but choosing to overlook it to completely abandoning me and cutting me out of the family was feasible. I knew the latter was the more extreme possibility, but I never thought that it would actually happen.

I'd always struggled to feel safe sharing my emotions with my parents, but even so, we were still a tight-knit family. We gathered for movie nights and pizza, we celebrated birthdays together, we spent holidays together, and on Christmas Eve, I still spent the night at my parents' house so we could all wake up under the same roof on Christmas morning.

We were there to help each other move, to see each other through medical procedures, and to enjoy family vacations in the mountains. Our family unit was strong, even if our relationships functioned on a superficial level. Coming out would definitely affect how we interacted with one another.

I knew it wouldn't be easy for my parents to accept that I was gay. It was going to take them some time to process and get on board. But considering our family dynamics, the way we were always present for each other's big (and small) victories, and the values my mom taught us growing up that family was more important than anything, I didn't expect my coming out to be as extreme as some of the horror stories I'd heard—of kids getting thrown out of the house and completely disowned. Instead, I reflected on the phrase my mom frequently told us as kids, "Friends will come and go, but your family will always be there for you." I clung to that and hoped it was true, because I knew life was about to get bumpy.

Still, I was nervous as hell. Like a film in constant repeat, my mind flashed through the range of things that *could* happen, playing scenes of all the possible outcomes over and over in my mind. The tension mounted to the point that not knowing how my family would react was causing more anxiety than actually knowing, and I couldn't handle it anymore. I wanted to get it over with so I could sleep at night without the daunting uncertainty of what was to come.

I thought long and hard about the best time and place to tell them. I didn't want it to be during a holiday or birthday celebration because, if it went poorly, it would mark that holiday forever. I didn't want to steal joy from another family member's special event by dropping the "gay" word like a bomb in the middle of a family vacation. I wanted it to be planned, thought-out, and purposeful. I didn't want to be impulsive and regret it later. Finally, when I knew I was ready, I told myself that the next time my brother was in town (he had moved out of state as part of a church-plant), I would get the family together and tell them.

When my brother then said he was coming for a visit in just a few weeks, the moment I dreaded was suddenly on the calendar. I tried not to panic, but I couldn't help it. I had no idea what this was going to mean for my life and my future.

Not long before I came out, my dad and I enjoyed a special evening together and attended a wine tasting. Alcohol was completely forbidden in our house when we were kids, but once Daniel and I were grown, Mom loosened the reins a bit and Dad occasionally enjoyed a glass of wine. The evening of our wine tasting was close enough to my coming out that I already harbored anxiety of what my future relationship with my dad would look like. I remember assuming the worst and thinking, "This could be the last time my dad and I ever do something like this together."

Little did I know that it actually would be.

• • • • •

The week before my brother came to visit I sat staring at my phone for an hour before finally mustering up the courage to call my mom. It rang and she answered. I tried to carry on a nonchalant conversation with small talk, but finally when there was a break, I said,

"Mom, I have something I'd like to talk to you, Dad, and Daniel about." Trying to come across as more confident than I actually felt, I continued, "I've been in counseling this past year working through some things, and I'd like to share some of my journey with you. Would you be willing to come to my house together this Saturday morning?"

My mom listened and hesitantly agreed to my vague request. I was sure to let her know that my counselor agreed to be there as well to answer any questions they might have, then quickly ended the conversation. After I hung up the phone, I sighed. It was set. April 14, 2012, was the day I would come out to my family. There was no going back now.

In an attempt to ground myself, I purchased a leather bracelet with a gold charm that read, "*Thou hast taught me to say, it is well with my soul.*" Those words from the famous hymn had long brought me comfort in troubling times. But now, they served as a constant reminder that regardless of the outcome, I could root my soul in the truth that all would be well.

I spoke with some of my affirming friends and made plans for them to sweep me away after the conversation with my family was over and take me to Denver for a "coming out celebration." I didn't know what was about to happen, but I knew that regardless of the outcome I would need to get

The bracelet I wore the day I came out

away, have some fun, and get my mind off things. I hoped the celebration would counteract whatever took place and be an expression of joy for being who I am and the brave step I had just taken.

As April 14 approached, I was edgy, irritable, anxious, restless, and terrified. Friends and even people I barely knew from Highlands kept telling me I was so brave to do what I was doing. But I didn't feel brave. In fact, I'd never felt more afraid of anything in my whole life. The fear was almost crippling.

My heart pounded like drums in my ears the morning of April 14th as I prepared for my family to arrive. I dressed up a little, so as to appear more confident than I actually felt inside. I wanted to present a calm but assertive approach to the conversation. I knew that if I left the door open for doubt, my family would see it as hope that I might change. I wanted them to know that I was resolute and at peace.

Tying my bracelet around my wrist, I heard a knock at the door. It was Morgan. True to her word, she showed up early to support me and be there for the family meeting.

In the few minutes we had together, I asked Morgan not to leave me alone after my family left, no matter how things went down. If the conversation went poorly, I didn't trust myself to stay safe. I didn't know what I might do. I asked her to stay until one of my friends arrived to drive me to Denver, and she agreed.

Then there was another knock on the door. My stomach now literally quivered inside me. I looked at Morgan with nervous fear, swallowed the lump in my throat, and forced a smile.

"Good morning," I welcomed as calmly as I could, opening the door and inviting each of my family members inside. Their good-morning remarks in reply were colder than normal. They were distant, guarded, almost as if they'd been prepped for the conversation. They clearly knew something was up.

I served them tea from the kitchen and they each took a seat on the couch across from me in the living room. Morgan sat quietly to the side—present, but not intrusive. Tension hung thick in the air.

Finally, after some very awkward small talk, I inhaled the deepest breath I could muster and began.

"Thank you for coming this morning. There's been a lot going on in my life for the past few years and I feel like I'm finally at a point where I'm ready to share a very intimate and personal part of my life with you. I've been seeing Morgan for counseling for a year now and she's helped me a lot on this journey I've been on. She offered to be here today for support.

"Mom and Dad, I'm sure you've wondered why I've been more distant from both of you lately. It's because I wanted to search out answers for myself before sharing details with you. And now that I have, there's a lot to catch you up on. It takes a lot of courage to be this vulnerable, so I'm asking that you please hear me out."

All three of them looked solemn and uncomfortable lined up next to one another on the couch. I glanced down at my notes for prompting, in hopes that it would give me strength. Then, seeing the bracelet wrapped around my wrist, I forced another deep breath, and started with some back-story.

"I know you're aware of what happened between Brooke and me several years ago, but a lot has happened since then . . ."

I explained my journey and all that had transpired from the time Brooke left to now. I spoke of the tremendous amount of condemnation, judgment, and self-hatred I'd suffered; how I felt so suffocated inside that it caused me to relapse back into cutting after almost five years of being cut-free. I was open and vulnerable, exposing as much of my heart as I felt safe to do in order to help them understand the road I had traveled. I talked about dating men, I told them about my time with Darius (leaving out the fact that we slept together), and I awkwardly told them about the woman I'd seen, trying to push past the obvious discomfort of sharing those words aloud with my own parents.

I reserved using the word "gay" until later in the conversation, knowing that once that word escaped my lips, they most likely wouldn't hear anything else I had to say. They already looked like a herd of deer in the headlights.

"I've tried to change, but I *can't*," I explained. Not wanting to appear weak, I continued. "I got to the point where I couldn't deny my attraction to women, so I decided to face it head-on. I heard too many horror stories of people who suppressed their same-sex attractions and got married to an opposite-sex partner out of pressure to conform. Their marriages later resulted in divorce because they couldn't escape the truth of their sexual orientation. But by then, so many more people were affected. I refused to let that be me and forced myself to look this in the face."

Blank looks of growing discomfort and concern continued to stare back at me, but I pushed on. I explained the research and studying I'd done, how I'd found Highlands Church, the happiness and peace I'd found in the supportive community there, and finally, how I'd reached the conclusion that being attracted to someone of the same gender wasn't wrong or in opposition to God's will. Then, with all the courage I could muster, I pushed the two words out of my mouth that would forever change my future.

"I'm gay," I said. "I'm attracted to women, and I have been for a long time. I can't change it. It's part of who I am. And I can't live a lie anymore."

I assured them that this experience had only drawn me closer to God, not further away, and that I was in a place of peace—free of guilt and shame. I explained that my close friends already knew, but that I hadn't told any other family yet out of respect for all of them. I wanted them to know first.

"I did already tell Betsy," I told my mom. "I felt she deserved to hear it from me herself and I knew she'd be a good source of support for you. But beyond that, you're free to tell or not tell whatever family or friends you want to. I'm not going to flaunt it, but I'm not going to hide anymore either."

"I don't expect you to agree or approve," I said. "I know it's taken me years to get to where I am and that it will take each of you time as well. But I love you enough to share this with you and not to hide it. I wanted to be honest and to let you know. I don't know what the future holds, but this is where I'm at. I'm gay and I'm at peace with that."

It is extremely disheartening to be in a room full of people and feel completely alone. But when those people in the room are your own family, the feeling is even more isolating. With my heart laid bare before them, I waited for them to respond.

Those few seconds of silence that hung in the air were the most vulnerable I've ever felt in my life. My exposed heart hung on display in front of my family waiting to see whether I would be embraced or rejected. By the stoic looks on their faces, my hope for acceptance was quickly waning.

The first words to break the silence were spoken in my mom's stern voice. "I don't approve of your lifestyle, Amber. Thank you for being honest with us but, we'll have to see what this means for the future of our family."

I tried to maintain my composure. The future of our family? What was that supposed to mean? I looked at my dad with hopeful apprehension. Finally, with pursed lips he said, "I have *nothing* to say to you right now." Turning to my mom, he informed her, "I'm ready to go," and stood up to leave.

"I love you, Dad," I said looking at him despondently, as if begging to hear those words reciprocated. But without even daring to look at me, his only reply was, "Thanks for the tea," and he walked out the door.

Once both my parents were outside, my brother was left with me in the room. He came over, gave me a hug and said, "I love you, Am." Then he too disappeared.

The sound of that door shutting behind them as they left felt like they were simultaneously slamming the door of my heart that I'd offered them. Frozen in shock, I looked blankly at Morgan, and then, in despair, collapsed into the chair behind me.

13

ORPHAN AMBER

Sitting with my head in my hands, I was devastated. I felt unloved and unlovable. I felt disowned. I felt rejected, and I knew there was no going back. It was like living a nightmare, and I desperately wanted to wake up. I wanted to be alone so I could fall apart. But true to her word, Morgan wouldn't leave until we knew one of my friends was on the way to get me.

Looking back, if I could do it differently, I think that I would. I thought I owed it to my parents to come out to them in person. I thought they deserved to hear it from me, and that telling them in person was more respectful and honest. But knowing what I know now, I wish I had written them a letter in order to shield myself from their initial reaction. One thing I've learned over the last five years is that protecting myself is more important than protecting them. A child shouldn't have to shield their own parents from the truth. For far too long, I had protected them to the cost and detriment of my own safety and mental health. But in the end, it really didn't make a difference or change anything. It wasn't until I finally learned to set boundaries for the sake of my own safety and sanity that I actually started finding some healing from all the hurt.

The look on their faces the day I came out to them is forever seared into my memory, and in the weeks that followed I gathered many more snapshots that are still stored in the filing folders of my mind. I wish I had fewer of them. Each of them is still so painful to recall that at times it feels more like a terrible dream than reality.

But at the time, I did what I thought was best, and now I had to live with the repercussions. All I knew is that I felt suffocated, and I was desperate to get out and away from it all. I anxiously waited for my friends to arrive and sweep me away to Denver.

They took me out for a coming-out celebration that evening. People I'd never even met came to show their support. Many, with similar struggles of coming out, consoled me with the news that, "It just takes time. Your parents will come around eventually." I hoped they were right. Even though everyone kept telling me how brave I was to come out to my parents the way I did, all I could think of was how horribly wrong it had all gone, and how my life would never again be the same.

The next morning, my friends dropped me off to the emptiness of my own apartment. Now that all the commotion of celebrating was over, reality started to set in. I felt thoroughly depressed. In retrospect, *that* is probably when I shouldn't have been left alone.

What I ended up loving even more than the coming out celebration that night was a "Coming Out" scrapbook one of my friends made for me as a form of encouragement. She and I collaborated to gather notes and pictures from everyone in my life who was affirming of my sexuality, and we pasted them

Dear Amber,   6-20-12
    To live as if the good news might be better
than we believed and that God is bigger than the
dimensions we assigned, And that it is
actually TRUE that "perfect love casts out
all fear because fear has to do with
judgement" ... Well to Actually choose to
     1JN 4:10
live like that, as if God really has the capacity
        to love us beyond anything we can
    imagine - is a huge but warranted
leap of faith, act of courage And expression
of love. You have leapt, you are in flight,
And while I'm sure it is scary it is Beautiful to see
              NOTHING BUT LOVE, MARK

Card given to me by Pastor Mark Tidd for my "Coming Out" scrapbook

Mark Tidd and me

into the book. It was a brilliant idea that ended up giving me strength in the months to come. Any time I needed reminding that I was loved just the way I am, I would sit on the floor, open up that scrapbook, and read all the encouraging notes my friends had written me. It brought me such comfort. I still cherish it to this day.

• • • • •

After seven long days of silence from my family, I received a phone call from my dad.

"Your mom and I aren't ready to speak to you yet, Amber," he said in a firm tone. "But I just wanted to let you know that you're no longer welcome to go to the conference in St. Paul with your mom next month. I know you've already paid for your plane ticket, and if you still want to visit your friend there, that's up to you. But you can't stay with mom at the hotel or attend the conference with her. And if you do still decide to go, you'll have to find someone else to watch Half Pint [my dog], because I won't do it. We'll let you know when we're ready to talk to you about this. Goodbye." And he hung up.

If I wasn't second-guessing my decision to come out before, I definitely was now. I'd hoped that they just needed some time to process what I told them, but now, it wasn't looking that way. I vacillated, wondering if I'd done the right thing. Maybe I shouldn't have told them after all. Maybe living a lie *was* easier than telling the truth. But the exhaustion I felt from having to filter everything I said convinced me that the double life would never have worked for me in the long run. I had to live open and honest, even if it cost me everything.

It was three weeks before my parents contacted me again, telling me they were finally ready to talk. Although it made me uncomfortable, I agreed to meet them at their house, rather than in public, so we could talk more privately. Settling into the family room in the basement that held so many fond memories for me, it was clear that this conversation wouldn't be pleasant.

My mom and dad sat side by side, presenting a strong, cohesive force. They prefaced the conversation with, "Before we say anything, Amber, you need to know that we love you. But . . ." and so it began. I'm not sure why Christians always feel the need to preface their harsh words with, "I love you" before telling you that you're wrong about something. The theory of tough love is a common one among Christians, and I'm sure Dobson's support of that theory influenced my parents a great deal. When it comes to the gay community specifically, Dobson said, "We are obligated as Christians to treat homosexuals respectfully and with dignity, but we are also to oppose, with all vigor, the radical changes they hope to impose on the nation. It is vitally important that we do so."[9]

In the same article Dobson also denies having ever done or said anything that would be harmful to the gay community. But encouragement from evangelical leaders to implement a tough love approach has been severely detrimental to many LGBTQ people, causing them to feel like they have to change an innate part of themselves in order to be acceptable to God. "Speaking the truth in love" is often used as a free pass that allows

---

9. Dr. James Dobson's Family Talk, *Speaking the Truth in Love.* http://drjames dobson.org/articles/courage-in-the-home/speaking-the-truth-in-love.

Christians to say whatever they want. As a result, it has driven many away not only from the church, but from a relationship with God.

That's what my parents were about to do: "speak the truth to me in love."

"I feel like you've died, Amber—like I've lost you," my dad began with a grievous look on his face. My mom agreed.

"I feel the same way. You've turned your back on God and everything we've ever taught you," she stated with resolve. Everything I'd told them three weeks ago about how much time I spent seeking God and searching the Bible, everything I'd said about how this whole process actually brought me closer to God, not further away, had been disregarded. They only heard what they wanted to hear.

"We're hurt that you didn't come to us with this sooner," my dad continued. "We would have loved to help you by sending you to a Love Won Out conference.[10] We would have loved to walk through this with you. Even if you still arrived at the same decision, at least we would have known that we did everything we could to persuade you. But because you didn't include us in your journey, it's too late. You've already made up your mind.

"But you're deeply deceived, Amber. Like Eve, you've eaten the fruit from Satan. You've gotten in with the wrong crowd and they've brainwashed you. You're putting your soul in jeopardy. I'm afraid that you're damning yourself to hell."

My dad went on to compare me to murderers, pedophiles, and bestiality.

---

10. Love Won Out was an ex-gay ministry started by Focus on the Family and later sold to Exodus International.

"If I want to just go and marry a donkey, is that okay? Or if I see a little kid and want to have sex with them, can I just go ahead and do that and act on whatever I feel? You could even get a bunch of murderers together to form their own church and just make that all okay!"

Their words shattered me. I was devastated by their attacks on me, their own daughter, and felt gravely misunderstood. I didn't know what to say. I was tongue-tied and ill-equipped to handle such accusations. I never imagined I'd hear such horrible and harsh words from my own parents.

As if pulling out her last resort, my mom stood up and walked across the room.

"I printed out a list you wrote of qualities you said you wanted in a husband." Throwing it at me, she said, "Can you honestly tell me that if you found a man with all these qualities, you wouldn't fall in love with him?"

"I don't know," I said, feeling trapped and backed into a corner.

"I know," she shot back. "You would!"

"You don't understand," I tried. "This is not who I am. Do you want me to just be alone and miserable all my life?"

"I'd rather you be miserable in this life, than be miserable in the next," my dad said.

"We had no idea this was coming, Amber," my mom went on. "We honestly thought you were going to tell us that you had worked through all this and were over it. It's extremely selfish of you to do something that makes you happy without thinking about how this would affect the family." I couldn't believe she was serious. How this would affect the family is *all* I'd thought about for months leading up to this conversation.

"You've put your dad's job at Focus in jeopardy," she continued. "And your brother, at the happiest time in his life, now has to make decisions he should never have to make." My brother was recently engaged, so I can only assume she meant that he'd have to decide whether to include me in, or even invite me to, his upcoming wedding.

"And your grandpa for years has looked forward to giving you his grandfather's pocket watch someday. But now, he can no longer do that because you're out from under his blessing. We can no longer do things to help you anymore. You've left our covering.

"Honestly, I don't know what holidays are going to look like in the future," she said. "I don't know if you'll even feel comfortable being around us anymore." I think the reality was the other way around—they weren't sure if they would feel comfortable having *me* around for the holidays or what that might look like.

Then my dad added, "If you ever have a girlfriend, she'll *never* be allowed in our house. That's something that will never change. We're not going to disown or abandon you. We want you to know the door is always open, if you ever turn around and change."

As their rebuke neared its end, my mom pulled out a book about a man who'd had same-sex attractions but was supposedly healed through ex-gay therapy. She asked if I'd be willing to read it. I responded with what I thought was the best answer I'd given to anything all night:

"Well, how about this, I'll read one of your books if you'll read one of mine?" offering what I thought was a fair compromise.

"No, I'm not interested in that!" my dad shot back.

"Well then," I said, "I'm sorry, but I'm not interested." I tried not to offend my mom. I even looked at the book and told her to let me know what she thought of it after she read it herself. But I let them know that I wasn't going to take and read it if they weren't willing to meet me halfway. It may have been the only strong response I had all night, but I was proud of myself for standing my ground.

Finally, after I'd been thoroughly reprimanded and ostracized, the conversation wrapped up. But as I went to leave, there was one final jab to my heart that made all of this very real. As I went to walk out the door, my dad asked for the key to their house back. The childhood home that I'd grown up in from the age of seven, the door that had always been open to me to come by whenever I needed was now locked, and I was left out in the cold. I was now an outsider, no longer welcome as part of the family. He said they no longer trusted me to have open access to their home.

Baffled, I removed the key from my keychain and handed it to him. I think he tried to soften the blow by saying "I love you" before closing the door, but I don't remember for sure. All I could feel was the hurt, the pain, and the rejection from those I cared about the most. I never expected my parents to be accepting or approve of the fact that I was gay, but for first time in my adult life I took the risk of completely trusting in their love for me as my parents, yet was met with rejection. In my hour of greatest need, my family abandoned me.

Arriving home, I opened my journal and in utter heartbreak wrote ten of the most painful words of my life:

My worst fear has come true: I've become an orphan.

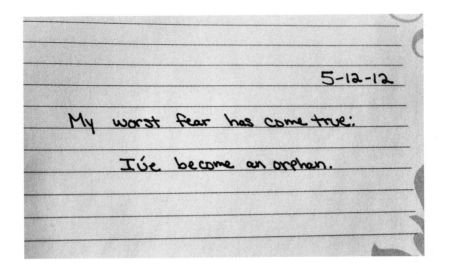

5-12-12

My worst fear has come true:

I've become an orphan.

I didn't know how my life would play out, but one thing was becoming clear. If I wanted to survive, I needed to move away from Colorado Springs.

14

THE PRICE OF LOVE

My phone rang unexpectedly, pulling me out of the only work assignment I'd taken for the last week and a half. I quickly excused myself and ran to the hallway where I could take the call. It was my brother.

"Amber, something's wrong with Dad. You need to get back to the hospital right away."

"Why? What's going on?" I asked in a panic.

"I don't know, but they're rushing him back in for emergency surgery. We need to get there fast!" he said, sounding equally anxious.

"I'm on my way!" I responded, hanging up the phone. I grabbed my things, quickly offered apologies to my coworkers through tears, and ran out the door.

• • • • •

That was the day I didn't know if I'd ever see my dad alive again. Only five months after coming out to my family, we had learned that my dad was gravely ill with a serious heart

173

condition. Open-heart surgery was required as soon as possible. Daniel flew in from out of state and, regardless of the awkwardness I'd felt around my family since coming out, I drove down from Denver to be present for the operation. Daniel and I both agreed to put our differences aside and do anything necessary to help get both our parents through this frightening and challenging time.

The surgery seemed successful at first, but as the week went on, Dad wasn't recovering the way we hoped he would, yet no one could figure out why. The doctors told us it might just take a little longer than predicted for him to heal. So one week post-op, they took him to run a series of tests before sending him home to finish his recovery. That's the day I decided to slip away for a few hours for a sign language interpreting assignment. It was the only time I'd left the hospital all week. Then I received the urgent call from my brother. The tests revealed what the problem was—Dad was within a few hours of losing his life.

By the time Daniel and I got back to the hospital, Dad was already being prepped for surgery again. Our fear was unspoken, but obvious—none of us thought Dad was strong enough to make it through surgery a second time. With heavy hearts, we all wondered if we'd see him alive again.

Once the nurse confirmed that he was back in surgery, we began the waiting process, just as we had done the week before. It was both surreal and uncomfortably familiar. In the quiet hours as we sat waiting for a verdict, I couldn't help but replay the events of recent months in my mind.

Loading the moving truck for Denver

•　•　•　•　•

It was only three months after coming out that I loaded up a moving van to start a new life in Denver. Taping up the final boxes, I could still hear the voices of my parents ringing in my ear.

> *"We would have loved to help you pick out a place and move to Denver, but because of why you're moving, we can't be involved."*

> *"I know you think this is what's best for you, but I have lived a lot longer than you, and I can tell you, this will not end well."*

"I'd rather you completely turn your back on God and be gay, than be gay and pretend like everything between you and God is okay."

Other repeated phrases like, "The door is always open *if* you ever change" and, "I love you, *but* . . ." made it clear that their love for me, when tested, came with strings attached.

I know they thought they were doing what was right. In time, they even tried to ask some leading questions like Focus on the Family advises.

What led you to believe that you might be gay?
How long have you struggled with this?
Will you tell me again about the journey that you've been on?

But so much damage was already done that I was not in a place to open up and be vulnerable with them again. I didn't feel they were truly interested in my journey as much as they wanted to use it as a gateway to help me change, or as my dad said, "fix things." My guard was up, and I couldn't share any more with them until I felt like they were truly trying to understand me, without a hidden agenda.

So many hurtful words followed behind me that day as I drove the moving truck from Colorado Springs to Denver, leaving behind the only hometown I'd ever known. Twenty years of memories were built in Colorado Springs. My whole life had been shaped and molded there.

Driving north on I-25 on my way out of town, a new life now awaited me. I didn't know what the future held; I just knew my future was no longer in Colorado Springs. I'd lived there too long to walk around unnoticed. Now that I was out, I didn't want to ever have to hide who I was again. I didn't want the anxiety that accompanied the constant watching and wondering what other people were thinking. I needed to be somewhere safe, somewhere fresh and new; somewhere I didn't have to hide. So I left behind a world full of memories for an uncertain future, hoping to find a sense of normalcy and belonging again.

In the months leading up to my coming out, I made sure everything was in place for me to financially survive on my own, just in case the worst should happen. Even though I'd been living on my own for almost ten years, my family and I still shared things like cell phone and insurance plans. I was financially independent; however, being self-employed meant money was tight, and moving to a new city only compounded that.

I scrimped and saved any way I could just to get by. I turned down parties because I couldn't afford a gift. I turned down coffee dates with friends because I couldn't spare the gas to get there. I skipped groceries I could get by without. I even returned groceries to the store a few times. Money was tight, and once I came out, I no longer had family to fall back on in case of an emergency. With my bank account dwindling and my credit card approaching the maximum limit, I hit bottom and found myself in tears the day I couldn't afford $1.98 for a gallon of milk.

Living paycheck to meager paycheck, with only catastrophic health insurance in place, I was completely dependent on God to provide. More than once, I saw his providence come through the provision of friends.

When I didn't have the full amount to put down on the condo I picked out in Denver, a member from Highlands

Church loaned me the advance with no questions asked. When I came down with pneumonia and kept willing myself to get better because I couldn't afford to go to the doctor, a choir friend handed me the needed cash and demanded I go. And when I desperately needed to learn and grow from a community of supportive Christians but couldn't afford the conference cost or travel fees, I was given a full-ride scholarship to attend. The generosity of my friends carried me through.

But still, living in a season of such uncertainty was frightening. I knew it would only take one thing going wrong to land me in a very dangerous and potentially homeless situation. It

Bonding with Half Pint during my darkest days

was humbling being forced to rely on God, on other people, and even on my dog to provide for my physical and emotional needs from day to day.

In the months leading up to and following coming out, my dog became my closest friend. She was my only loyal companion, and I gladly fed her before I fed myself. She was my one source of joy and the one constant I could count on to be there and love me unconditionally day after day. We bonded in a way that only those who have grieved deeply could understand.

• • • • •

I felt like so much of my life was out of my control during that time, and that's exactly how I was feeling again as I sat in the waiting room of the hospital—out of control. Although I was sitting right next to my mom and brother, I felt alone. We were joined together by fear of what was taking place in the operating room, but the added layer of my recent coming out set me apart. It was painful to acknowledge that I was still there for them, even when they failed to be there for me. Though the four of us as a family still shared the same blood, there was now an obvious division between the three of them (Mom, Dad, and Daniel), and me. Subtle cues in recent days made it even more obvious when my mom chose Daniel to be the first to visit Dad in the post-op room after the first surgery instead of me, or when we both arrived at their house the day before the operation and she gave Daniel the newly remodeled guest room and put me on a blow-up mattress in the basement. The message was clear: I was no longer equal to Daniel in their eyes.

Indirect manipulation and passive-aggressive behavior became the tactic my family chose in an attempt to get me to change. Rather than agreeing to disagree, they silently punished me. One of the most hurtful examples was when they planned an entire family vacation without me and then invited me for only part of the trip. Despite how their exclusion made me feel, I tried to remain consistent and decided to join them for a couple of days. I still wanted to prove to them that I was the same person they'd always known and loved. But when I arrived, I was told to sleep on the pullout couch instead of on the extra bed in the room where my future sister-in-law was staying. Their actions quietly shunned me and pushed me further and further to the outside. I felt like the family misfit, the black sheep, the outcast, the leper.

My mom continued to make comments like, "I know that deep down you know what you are doing is wrong," or "I have always spoken truth into your life and I will continue to do so, because I truly love you. It may not always be what you want to hear, but hearing the truth can be tough."

Although my dad and I weren't talking as often, his words sent in an email were equally painful, when he spoke of how embarrassed he was by me.

I could tell you that this isn't embarrassing Amber, but I'd be lying. It's very embarrassing. You made a choice that completely contradicts everything your mom and I taught you and know to be true. It stands opposite my life's work and the tenets of my employer. It is contrary to what Christians from the days of the first Church have held to be true. People look at me with certain expectations, and they have expectations that my family members will live according to the same principles that I've taught and believed. So I am troubled by the message this sends to hundreds of thousands of fans, and I am embarrassed by it. And this embarrassing situation hurts me. It hurts Mom, and it hurts everyone who has loved you and invested in you all these years. That it hurts you is sorrowful to me as well, but you made a conscious decision to pursue this lifestyle so you cannot blame us for the consequences of your choice.

These comments from my parents made it clear that if I wanted to feel loved, I had to play by their rules. And if I felt ostracized, it was my own fault—those are the consequences of sin. The fact that he couched the ending with another "I love you more than you know" didn't matter. Every "I love you" they spoke was drowned out by their hurtful words and lack of empathy and understanding. It was hard for me to believe I was becoming so estranged from my own family when we'd once been so close.

But the proof that it was real sat in the awkwardness between us in the hospital waiting room and in the ways I'd been treated since I'd been there. They were appreciative of my help. In fact, I don't think they expected me to come, so it surprised them that I was there supporting them for as long as I was. But still, there was an obvious discomfort between us.

· · · · ·

In the months since moving to Denver, I'd flourished in my new environment. I was finally appreciated and valued for who I was. It felt good to no longer live in my family's shadow. I was asked to be involved in leadership at church and joined a community choir where one of my original songs was performed and recorded in concert. Finally people were seeing me for the gifts

Performing with Highlands Church Choir at Denver PrideFest

I brought to the table. Out from under the shadow of other people, I was able to let my own personality and talents shine.

But everything wasn't perfect. Friends were vanishing; many people who initially showed love and support grew distant over time. I wanted to fight to maintain each and every one of those relationships, but it became overwhelming. The silence I received from some stung just as much as the hurtful words I received from others.

A few have watched my life quietly from a distance for enough time to now see the positive light shine through. They've seen how happy I am, how much joy I've found, and how at peace I've become. They may not say much, but I know that by living my life openly and consistently in front of them, I'm bearing witness of God's love to those who are watching.

Recently, I got an unexpected, handwritten letter in the mail. It was from a friend and former coworker of mine.

Dear Amber,

I have been thinking about what I have learned from our friendship. We've both faced uncharted waters together and I am incredibly grateful for the experience. I remember how honored I was when you opened up and told me you are gay. I was so sad for all the persecution you faced from family and friends.

But what really rocked my boat was when you told me you were getting married. I didn't realize it up until that point, but somewhere in my mind I had formed this opinion that we could be friends, but if you decided to get married, that changed everything. I just didn't know what to do. I'm sorry my decision to not attend your wedding hurt you.

Since then, I have thought a lot about my friends who are gay. Who am I to put conditions on friendship? The Savior never said, "I only love you if. . . ." He showed the way of unconditional love. That's the kind of love I want to have not only for my family, but my friends as well. Who am I to say, "I'll love you only if you live within the boundaries I want"?

I want you to know how much I love you. Even if our religious and family beliefs differ, you are still Amber. To love you is to accept who you are and your family.

Seeing how divided our country has become, I feel an even more urgent need to make sure I'm building bridges. Together

our differences can unite us if we will choose love—uncondi-
tional love. Better tomorrows start with building and main-
taining friendships to last a lifetime.

   Lots of love,
   Emmalee

This letter took so much courage and humility to write. It meant so much to know that by allowing my friend to quietly observe my life from the sidelines, I'd influenced her understanding and definition of love. It's beautiful and it's encouraging.

But then there are people, like my grandmother, who felt the need to take a more overt stand. On several occasions following my coming out, though she was pleasant and kind to me in person, she then followed up our visit with an email like this:

In today's world Amber, it is very difficult to see a grand-
child being deceived. We cannot twist Scripture to justify how
we want to live. I know you well enough to know that in
your heart, you know better than this. But I can tell that you
are very determined to go ahead with it, even though not one
single member of your family agrees with you. Satan always
comes as an angel of light and you are letting a worldly view
cheat you out of God's best for your life. God is a God of love
and mercy and forgiveness, but He is also a God of wrath and
punishment for disobedience.

   I love you Amber, but [there it was again, that "but"], I
cannot condone what you are doing. If I didn't love you, I cer-
tainly would not speak so openly to you. I am concerned for
your very soul. If this was of the Lord, it would not separate
you from all those who love you and have invested in your life.

You see, your family is always your family, but friends come and go.

I thought back to the countless times my mom had told me that very thing growing up.

"Amber, friends will come and go, but your family will always be there for you." I realize now that she'd learned that from her own mother. But as I looked around, I didn't see a single family member being there for me. Even as we waited for the results of my dad's unexpected surgery, my friends were the ones checking in, driving down from Denver to visit, and making sure I was okay. These friends were being there for me, even as my blood relatives sat uncomfortably beside me.

• • • • •

After several hours went by, unable to wait any longer, Daniel went to the nurse's desk asking for an update. She checked with the doctor and informed us that they were still in surgery, but that it shouldn't be much longer. I thought about the surgeon who was sewing up my dad's ribcage for the second time in a week. I prayed for him, and for Dad. I thought of how tender and painful the recovery would be if he survived.

It hadn't been long ago that I feared I myself might not survive. With nightmares of how my family treated me invading my sleep night after night, my depression was worsening. This was the lowest point of my life. At every other turning point, there was always a light at the end of the tunnel that pushed me forward somehow. But for the first time, I felt like that light had been extinguished. I couldn't see things getting better; I couldn't find hope, and as I searched for a reason to keep living,

I could no longer find one. I felt consumed by hopelessness. Suicide was beginning to feel like my only real option.

I confided in my mom one day how suicidal I felt. Her emailed response was this:

I hope and pray you would never do something so selfish, Amber. But let's look at this: you announce that you are gay, move away, choose to surround yourself with all new friends, family, and church members knowing all along what we believe, what we stand for, and what our convictions are. And then it is our fault? That would be like Dad having an adulterous affair and then coming to me and saying that it's just who he is—he can't change, he is going to continue to have that affair, and I need to accept that. Then he tells me that he almost committed suicide because I couldn't accept the fact that he was living in adultery. Are you kidding me? You are NOT the victim here. If anyone has reason to feel desperate, it's me.

These are the most painful words my mom's ever said to me. She downplayed my pain, made light of my life's value, and made committed same-sex marriages equivalent to adultery. She ignored my cry for love and failed to recognize the fact that their slow shunning of me is what was pushing me to the edge of suicide.

I began making end-of-life plans. Who could I trust to take care of my faithful companion—my dog, Half Pint? Who would I leave my possessions to? I didn't have much, but my journals and scrapbooks had always been precious to me and both held intimate pieces of my heart. I wondered who would care for them if I couldn't survive. My days were dark and long as I struggled with thoughts of death and wondered if I'd make it through.

There were so many moments when I wanted to give up on hope—days I was convinced that I couldn't continue if something didn't change. But for some reason, hope just wouldn't give up on me. In my lowest of low moments, I'd get a text from someone checking in to see how I was doing, or a church member would hug me in a way that showed they knew what I was feeling, even without saying a word, or Half Pint would cuddle up right beside me as if to say, "You just can't leave. I need you."

Half Pint was there when everyone else walked out. Her unconditional love is what kept me going on my hardest and loneliest days. She was always excited to see me every time I walked through the door, and no matter what my day was like, she stayed by my side. We depended on each other to survive, and somehow, that was enough to carry me through those darkest days when it seemed there was no other reason for living.

· · · · ·

I was quickly pulled away from my thoughts and back to the waiting room as I saw the surgeon, still in his scrubs, walking toward us. All three of us immediately stood in tense anticipation.

"He's alive," the doctor said, hearing us collectively breathe a sigh of relief. "We drained ten liters of fluid from around his heart and lungs. He's very weak, but we found the root of the problem and the surgery was successful."

"Thank God," Mom whispered. "Can we see him?"

"He's in ICU and I want to keep him there for several days. You can see him, but only two at a time."

"Thank you doctor," Daniel said, giving the doctor a firm handshake.

"Yes, thank you," I chimed in. "You saved his life."

"It was a close call," the doctor replied. "If we hadn't caught it when we did, I don't think he would have made it through the day."

Tears welled in our eyes with the thought of how close we'd come to losing him, coupled with the relief of knowing he'd survived the surgery a second time.

· · · · ·

It was only a couple hours later that I stood in the ICU room, holding my dad's hand. Still heavily sedated and on a ventilator, he wasn't alert, but I tried to let him to know I was there. Then, despite all the tubes he was connected to, and all the machines that were aiding his recovery, he managed to find a way to send me a message. Taking me by surprise (it had been a long time since we'd used this secret code), he gently squeezed my hand three times. It was the silent signal we'd used all our lives to say, "I love you."

With tears in my eyes, I said, "I love you too, Dad," and squeezed his hand in return.

15

THE TURNING POINT

A full month passed before my dad was well enough to come home from the hospital. The doctors released him just ten days before my brother got married. I wish I could say that my dad's near-death experience somehow changed his view of me and my sexuality, but it didn't. Of course I didn't take care of him with the expectation that he would accept me, but I did hope during those weeks that my consistent presence might cause him to see me as the daughter he'd always known, and prompt him to reevaluate what's truly important. But even as his frail body struggled to heal, his resolve was unchanged in his stance toward me. Once he arrived home, our relationship quickly returned to its awkward and distant state.

I was disappointed, but not just with him. I was also disappointed in Christian institutions like Focus on the Family and New Life Church. I felt like they had failed me. In the time that I needed someone to love me and be Jesus to me the most, their tough love approach taught my family and friends to distance themselves rather than embrace me. Their comfort took priority over my inclusion and their fears won out over my need for love. The importance of family that Focus taught, the value of community that New Life modeled, and our personal family motto that, "Friends will come and go but your family will always be there for you," disintegrated when I came out and left me feeling alone, even in presence of family.

· · · · ·

It was only a couple months later that a phone call once again pulled me away from work. This time it was my mom. I knew something must be wrong since she rarely called me anymore. Excusing myself from the room, I stepped into the hall to take the call. I feared that my dad had experienced a setback of some kind, but instead, I heard my mom's voice coldly tell me that my favorite Grandpa Henry had suffered a heart attack and passed away earlier that afternoon. Another wave of grief washed over me and threatened to pull me under.

"Am I *ever* going to catch a break?" I wondered. Grandpa Henry and I had shared a close bond from the time I was a toddler. All through my teen years and even into adulthood, we maintained a strong relationship. I loved singing old country gospel songs with him as he played his guitar, and had many fond summer memories of visiting him throughout the years. I still remember the countless times he'd looked at me with a smile and said, "I love you, Amber. I really do."

But his love, like the love of my parents, also shifted when he heard of my coming out. Although he never spoke to me about it directly, my mom made sure I knew that he was disappointed in me. Daniel's wedding was the last time I saw him.

The knowledge of how he now viewed me made our interaction uncomfortable. Warmth was replaced with unspoken tension. I knew Daniel's wedding wasn't the time to have that conversation with Grandpa Henry, but I do regret that I never got around to it before he died. I wanted him to see and understand my heart, but now it was too late.

· · · · ·

So much took place within that first year of coming out—so many differing degrees of transition and loss. It's no surprise that my PTSD significantly worsened during 2012. Every time I look back at all that year held for me, I wonder how I survived. Not only did I come out and move to Denver, but we also experienced the grave illness of my dad, my brother's wedding, and the passing of Grandpa Henry. Attending these life-altering events was not optional in my mind, yet they took a serious toll on me. So much was going on beneath my smile that other people couldn't see.

I finally decided to speak with my doctor about training Half Pint to become a service dog. She had been instrumental in my healing. She was my lifeline. My medical records clearly indicated my long history of PTSD, and with all the additional trauma that 2012 had held for me, my doctor wholeheartedly approved.

I began training Half Pint in her new role. She was overstimulated in public places at first, but she soon adjusted and was calm and content as long as I was near. The bond already formed between us made it easy for her to learn to recognize my anxiety and PTSD triggers. She wore her purple vest with

Half Pint becomes a service dog

pride, knowing that putting it on meant she was working to help me. With PTSD being covered under the Americans with Disabilities Act, Half Pint was soon qualified to have full access as a service dog everywhere I went. She became (and still is) my companion when my anxiety is high or when I attend certain events that are potentially triggering.

I now realize that training Half Pint to be a service dog and moving to Denver were the two best decisions I made during that time. The ability to have a fresh start in a new city, combined with the support I found at Highlands Church, and the unconditional love and assistance of Half Pint, is indeed what saved my life. I took small steps forward each day, and eventually, a new year rolled in. I had never been so eager to mark the end of a year before. Thankfully, as I entered 2013, my life finally turned a corner.

• • • • •

I'll never forget the first time I attended the Gay Christian Network (GCN) conference. Hundreds of people from across the country migrated to Phoenix for the weekend to share in fellowship and gain a deeper understanding of what it means to be both gay and Christian. There was so much love, freedom, and acceptance there that my mind was on overload.

During one workshop, I made a comment during the Q&A that caught the ears of a particular man in the room. Later that evening, he came up to me and said, "Hi, my name is Mike. This is my wife, Loretta. Can we take you to dinner?"

Surprised and a little perplexed by this invitation from a complete stranger, I wasn't sure what to think, but said, "Okay," followed by a smile. With little more information than that, I got in the car with a couple I'd never met and we all headed out for a meal together.

Sitting around the table, an almost instant bond was formed as we shared our stories with one another. I told them about my upbringing as the daughter of a Focus executive, about my coming out, and about the devastation I'd faced in recent months. They shared a very similar experience, but in reverse. They told me that two of their four daughters were gay, and that after ten years of struggle, they were trying to embrace full inclusion and acceptance of them.

Our willingness to be vulnerable in that space exposed an unrealized need that lay dormant inside each of us. I desperately needed to feel love and acceptance from a Christian parental figure. They needed a Christian gay daughter to learn from. Our need for each other fused our hearts together and created a special bond that continues to this day. I didn't know it at the time, but in the years to come, they would end up filling a lot of the holes in my heart from my own parents' absence, including the day I married my wife.

Attending GCN that weekend was like crossing a threshold for me. I was inspired by the many other gay Christians I saw who had walked similar journeys. It helped me feel less alone. I was encouraged by the stories I heard from the people who shared publicly about their shifts in theology. It further confirmed that I wasn't deceived the way so many family and friends had said. I was hopeful because of the parents I'd met, like Mike and Loretta, that maybe someday things would get better for me too. This was the beginning of 2013, and with the turn of this new year, strength and health started taking root in my heart. It still took a lot of time to mend from all of the trauma, but I was gradually gaining some footing, which in turn provided some breathing room to heal.

• • • • •

Not long after attending GCN, I woke up on a Sunday morning in February to a huge blizzard. The snow was deep, and I doubted whether I could even make it out of the parking lot, much less to the other side of town for church.

"Isn't this just my luck," I thought. "It would have to blizzard on the one day that I'm supposed to share my life story at Community Hour." Community Hour at Highlands Church was like a form of Sunday school, and Life Stories rotated throughout the group once a month in order to better know and understand each other's journeys.

This morning was my turn. As if I weren't already nervous enough about sharing my personal struggles publicly to this group of church people, now it had to dump three feet of snow. I was convinced I'd show up and see only four or five people sitting around one round table waiting to hear me—people who already knew my story because they'd walked it alongside me. Frustrated and a little bitter about the timing of this storm, I almost postponed my talk. But instead, I prepared myself for disappointment as I drove the icy roads to church and walked down the hall to the room where Community Hour was held. Stepping into the doorway, I stopped. Before me sat a room full of people—people who cared about me so much that they'd shoveled their driveways, scraped off their cars, and driven to church just to hear me share my story. Overwhelmed by their support, I broke down in tears.

After taking a minute to collect myself, I began. I shared my growing-up years, passing around childhood photos for people to see varying versions of my cute three-year-old and seven-year-old self. I spoke of my journey through faith and sexuality and the turmoil I'd faced the previous year in light of coming out. And I took the opportunity to publicly thank many of them who had personally supported me in my journey along the way.

Sharing my story publicly for the first time was a powerful moment. It strengthened not only my confidence, but also my ability to live authentically in front of people, without hiding behind masks of perfection. It was freeing to finally show all of who I was in front an audience, without parts of me being forced to silently hide from the public eye.

At the end of the talk, a woman came up to me, introduced herself as Clara, and returned the childhood photos I'd passed around. Chatting briefly and, quite frankly, not thinking anything of it, I then turned to the next person waiting to speak with me. I had no idea how carefully Clara had been listening to my story, and was certainly oblivious to the fact that she was especially intrigued when learning that I was not only gay, but also Christian, and single. My life was about to take a drastic turn yet again, but this time for the better. For that woman I'd just met was the woman I'd fall in love with, and one day call my wife.

16

LOVE LOST, LOVE GAINED

There were two things my mom always told me about meeting the love of my life. The first was that meeting the right person often happens when you least expect it. And she was right. I had no idea when I shared my story at Community Hour that Sunday in February 2013, that one of the women listening was not only falling in love with my story, but also falling in love with me. The start of our relationship definitely came in a season when I least expected it.

The second thing my mom always told me about relationships was that when you find the right person, the relationship can move along very quickly. While I know my relationship with Clara isn't what my mom had in mind when she said that, this statement also proved to be true. If you asked Clara, I'm certain she would agree that she knew we were meant to be together even before I did. But once we started dating, I soon caught up to her. We both knew fairly quickly that our relationship was heading toward a commitment of marriage. It was a season of excitement, of falling in love, and of discovering new parts of who I was and what I had to give. Having not dated much, and being secretive about my relationship with Brooke, this was the first time I was ever able to publicly call someone mine. Introducing her as my girlfriend added a level of joy because it was representative of the fact that things were finally the way they were meant to be.

One thing I loved about Clara was that she was nothing like Brooke. She was stable, she was consistent, and she was mature. With a high level of education, Clara has served her country in the Army, and held down the same job in the same place for a long time. I was impressed by the fact that she was stable and established. Having known she was gay since she was five, Clara's sexuality was not new to her. And as first-generation Filipino, she was used to living in the margins of diversity as an Asian, gay, Christian woman in the military. She came out much earlier than I did and I found comfort in her commitment to being both true to herself and to her relationship with God.

From day one, she treated me well. I felt loved, respected, and valued when we were together. And most importantly, she made me feel safe. It wasn't just a superficial safety, but a safety in the deepest parts of my heart where it really mattered.

I remember the day I told Clara I had TTM.

"I have something to tell you," I said to her on the phone. Even though many years had passed since my diagnosis, nerves still turned my stomach any time I talked about my hair-pulling disorder. I knew I needed to tell her, but how she reacted was critical for our relationship, and that made me anxious.

"I'll send it in an email," I told her, using email as a cop-out to calm my butterflies. I typed out what I felt she needed to know, wrote *My Deepest Insecurity* in the subject line, and hit "Send."

Trusting her with something that I still struggled with and continued to carry deep embarrassment over was a pivotal point for us that tested our compatibility. She responded with nothing but kindness, love, and understanding. That was one of many moments that told me I was safe with her.

Finding safety in Clara was priceless. It meant not only did I no longer have to be physically lonely, but I also no longer had to suffer the emotional loneliness that I'd faced for so many years.

Everything about our relationship felt so right and so beautiful. Even in moments of disagreement or conflict, there was a level of commitment between us that created a haven of safety allowing us to both be ourselves and share our burdens. There was a simple freedom about it that grounded me, even when my family relationships continued to be hard.

I wanted so much to be able to share this new and exciting part of my life with my parents. I wanted to celebrate this season with them and for them to get to know Clara. But sadly, the longer that Clara and I dated, the more my relationship with my parents eroded.

My dad told me that when it came to holidays, I would always be welcome in their home, but Clara would never be allowed under their roof. It grieved me deeply that we couldn't share holidays together the way we once did, but going without Clara was never an option to me. I told him that saying she wasn't welcome was the same as saying that I'm not welcome. I put it in perspective by reminding him that he would certainly never go somewhere for the holidays where Mom wasn't allowed. I never asked them to agree with our relationship, but

I did ask that they treat both Clara and me with respect, both as human beings and as adults. But they struggled to do that.

I tried to let go of my need for their approval, but it was hard. Their pride over my accomplishments had carried me through a good portion of my life. My people-pleasing nature wanted them to be proud of me for the milestones I was achieving. But I ultimately realized that I had to let go of that ideal and start setting boundaries with them in order to protect myself.

Setting boundaries with my parents was not something I was used to. Honoring your father and mother was an important value in our home and setting boundaries with them was often mistaken for disrespect. That meant it was just as hard for them to accept the boundaries I set as it was for me to set them. Although it was difficult, the longer that Clara and I knew each other, the more secure I felt in her love, and that love then empowered me, over time, to refocus my family.

· · · · ·

After eight months of dating, getting to know one another, laughing together, and creating memories of our own, Clara and I were engaged. We knew this was only the beginning of what we wanted to be a lifetime of sharing in each other's journeys. While it seemed quick to some, we felt ready. We were both well into our adult lives so, to us, there was no reason to prolong what we already knew we wanted and felt God was blessing.

We started making announcements and planning for the big day. Excitement rose. Venues, dates, color schemes, the wedding party, and more all spun like a whirlwind. I planned endlessly. It had both its moments of euphoria and extreme stress.

Clara and I get engaged

Anyone who's ever planned a wedding knows what I mean. It's utter chaos.

The daunting task of telling my parents we were engaged felt like the equivalent of a second coming out. I knew for them, it would solidify what, up until that point, they'd hoped would still change. It took me so long to finally muster the courage to tell them, that sadly, they ended up being among the last to know. Joy was flourishing in my life, and I didn't want that joy to be smothered by further disapproval. I finally felt truly happy and I wanted a chance to soak it up.

When I finally did tell my parents that Clara and I were engaged, I received a ten-page letter from my mom detailing her heartbreak and despair over the direction my life had taken.

What I wish my parents were able to see is that, if they put gender aside, Clara is everything they could ever want for me. She is the embodiment of what they prayed all my life for me to find in a spouse. The package didn't come wrapped the way they expected it to, but the contents are the same. She has high morals and values. She maintains her integrity. She loves God. She works hard. She respects and loves me deeply. She's kind, she's loving, she's selfless. What more could they want for me?

When Clara and I were married and we moved into our first home, I went through all the boxes that held childhood mementos. Tucked inside an old journal, I found a list of character traits I desired in my future husband that I had crafted around the age of sixteen. Reading down the list, I found that Clara fit almost every one of them. It was validating. To me it was proof that, regardless of what other people said or believed, my own integrity and values remained intact.

Obviously, my views on diversity, inclusion, and equality have changed from the mindset in which I was raised. But many other things that I loved and valued prior to coming out are still alive in my heart. Unfortunately, my parents couldn't see that. They still believe that I have strayed from God and from everything they raised me to believe and that with enough prayer, one day I will return to the foundation I was grounded in as a child. My mom once told me that she does not believe anyone is born gay:

"I believe something happens along the way to confuse or hurt them that makes them turn to homosexuality for the affection and love they so desire. I do not despise you or any gay person. I do despise Satan, who is a deceiver and is leading so

Character Traits of My Future Husband (Age 16)

- Holds me to living a life of high standards + strong morals.
- Inspires me in my walk with God
- Is my very best friend & I, his.
- Is a servant to the end.
- Will support + stand by me in what I believe + do.
- Stands up for what he believes + doesn't follow the crowd
- Is wise + real / authentic.
- Loves to be involved at church + serve.
- Protects me + makes me feel safe.
- Maintains open lines of communication in our relationship.
- Is understanding of my past + will protect my weak spots.
- Cultivates a high level of trust in our relationship.
- Loyal not matter what the circumstances.
- Laughs easy (and often)
- Loves to have a good time
- Thinks I'm beautiful, even when I've just gotten out of bed.
- Knows how to play hard + work hard.
- Loves God first, + me second.

*List of character traits I desired in my future
husband at the age of sixteen*

many astray. But, I also believe we serve an amazing God who forgives all of our sin, heals all of our diseases, and helps us gain victory over them."

I wish my parents didn't see me as confused and wounded. I wish they didn't see my relationship with Clara as sinful and diseased. But even amidst all the hurt from the rejection, there's a part of me that is sad for them—sad that they are unable to see God outside of the small box and set of rules so many Christians have forced him into. They have no idea that God came not only to shatter that box, but to make the world even more beautiful with its diversity.

At the end of the long letter my mom wrote, she told me that she has an angel named Hope that holds a candle sitting on her coffee table in honor of me. She said that every time she sees it, she prays for my return: a return to myself, to my family, to my friends and loved ones, and to my foundation. She vowed to leave it there always until I return to them. She promised she would never give up hope, and prays that I return sooner rather than later. But regardless, she will always be waiting for my return with open arms.

Yes, it hurt to read this. But it also makes me feel for them, because I'll never be able to return to them the way they hope I will. I've met so many incredible people over the last five years—people who have walked hard roads to get to where they are, but are so raw, humble, and authentic because of it. These people are inclusive, willing to learn, and open to embracing the beautiful diversity of God in all its forms, even when some of them are hard to understand. These are the kind of people I have longed to meet all my life.

Having finally found these people, and being unwilling to ever hide pieces of me again for the sake of appearance has made me realize that I could never go back to where I came from. Rather, my parents would have to come to me. They would have to arrive at a place of humility where they were willing to embrace diversity, and open their minds to learn about different experiences and viewpoints. I don't know what it will take for them to arrive at that place—perhaps brokenness, perhaps humility, perhaps letting go of control and appearances, or perhaps simply time. But what I do know is that I refuse to ever wear a mask again in order to make other people comfortable, even when those people are my family.

• • • • •

One of the hardest things I've ever had to do is plan my wedding, knowing that my family wouldn't be there. My parents refused even to meet Clara when we were dating. After telling them Clara and I were engaged, my mom made it clear that, at a time when she should be rejoicing, she was grieving. She told me that she was unable to share in the wedding-planning process because she could not go against her convictions and support the choices I was making.

"I want you to understand why," she said. "I believe that God clearly lays out in his Word that marriage is to be between one man and one woman. Marriage is a holy sacrament put in place by God to signify and represent the church as his Bride. That is what the entire foundation of Christianity was built on and if we lose that, we lose everything. I love you, but sometimes love is very hard."

There are two things I learned from that statement. First, whether she realizes it or not, my mom is afraid—afraid that if she condones my relationship with Clara, it will put a crack in her belief system that will spread, causing her entire foundation of faith to crumble. That fear is very real. I remember facing it myself and thinking, "If I'm wrong about *this*, what else am I wrong about?" It's terrifying to feel like the entire foundation you've built your life upon is being shaken. It takes incredible strength and courage to walk that path in faith, despite the trembling ground, and face that life-altering fear head-on.

But the other thing that came through loud and clear in that statement was her belief that love must be tough and hard. And it *was* hard. The way they chose to love me was hard for me as well as for them. I recognize that being gay and marrying

Clara is not the direction they saw my life going. I can even sympathize with the fact that they've had to grieve many of the dreams they had for me. I've had to grieve many of those dreams as well, not because my dreams have changed, but because they lacked my family's presence in them. The wonderful couple I met at GCN, Mike and Loretta, even offered to speak to my parents on my behalf. They wrote a beautiful letter telling them a little of their own journey with a gay daughter and offering to talk with them in more detail. But my dad turned them down flat. He said he already knew the truth about what God said on this topic and didn't care to discuss it further.

So I knew there was no way they would even consider attending our wedding. They would not let their presence show support for a commitment of love they saw as shameful. And yet, an invitation with their name and address sat on my kitchen table for weeks, as my broken heart so deeply wished that things were different. Everyone should have the love and support of their parents on their wedding day.

But our relationship was so turbulent that I knew their presence would *not* be comforting. And that realization was equally painful to knowing they refused to have any part in our lives. Our wedding was a sacred moment, one I had looked forward to all my life. Clara and I were so happy together. I felt whole and free. I couldn't wait to give my life to her before God, family, and friends. And my heart ached and longed for my relationship with my parents to be in a place where they could celebrate that with us. But it was not.

Every time I thought about my parents attending the wedding, my anxiety intensified. Fear of my family showing up at the ceremony with intervention plans provoked nightmares unlike any I'd ever experienced. Deep sobs from intense heart-ache repeatedly woke me in the midnight hours.

All along I tried hard never to lash out in anger, never to say things I might regret, or that could be used against me. I tried to be calm but firm in the boundaries I set. I fought to maintain connection during holidays and birthdays, attempting to show them I was still the same person and that they were still important to me. But over time, it became exhausting. The constant anticipation and wondering what to do for that birthday, or how to handle this holiday, drained me of all my emotional energy. It became toxic. I tried to keep a wall up around my heart to prevent them from seeing how much damage they'd actually done, but in hindsight, I wish they had seen more of it.

Even though in 2012 I worked hard to maintain contact with my family as much as possible and cultivate a sense of normalcy, that waned in 2013 as Clara and I met and started dating. Conversations between my parents and me went from cold to icy. By the time Clara and I were engaged and planning our wedding, my relationship with my parents had disintegrated almost completely.

Eventually, I ended up removing all family from my Facebook account. I'd fought against doing that for a long time. It felt like it was the last window into their lives that still remained. But Clara could see what it was doing to me. While that final string kept me connected to them, it also served as a constant reminder that I was the outcast of the family. Photo streams on my wall of holidays I should have been a part of, and family vacations I should have been included in, each left me feeling more ostracized. My mom posted her pride over her daughter-in-law and the time they spent together the way she previously used to brag about me. I felt replaced. It ate me up inside. I finally had to cut the tie and let it go.

Our conversations became less frequent as the wedding drew near. I didn't mention it. They didn't ask. But mostly, we just didn't talk. All the other areas of my life were so filled with joy. It angered me that family disagreements tainted this beautiful season. Ironically, the more distant our relationship became, the better I handled it. Not that it hurt any less, but it gave me some room to breathe and begin healing.

Not long before ties were completely cut between me and my parents, I hit a point where I'd felt backed into a corner for so long, that I finally told them in a letter exactly how all their comments and treatment affected me. I'd heard countless times all the ways I'd disappointed them, how embarrassed they were by me, and how my choices were sinful and putting my soul at risk. I owed it to them, and more importantly, to myself, to tell them the ramifications of *their* behavior.

I was respectful, but direct and honest. I no longer minced words. I knew it would come across as harsh, but I was no longer willing to absorb their abusive words and say nothing. I deserved respect. I was tired of being bullied by my own family into believing and doing what they thought was right, and I called them on it. At the end of my letter, out of my deepest pain and anger, I told them, "If you love me, prove it—because right now, I don't believe you."

Those were the harshest words I'd ever spoken to my parents. But I needed them to know that what they perceived as love was really just an excuse for their bullying behavior.

As expected, everything I said fell on deaf ears. The only response I got to everything I expressed was, "I'm sorry you feel that way. I hope someday you will understand the reason for our decisions, and come to know how much we truly do love you."

That was one of the last times I spoke to my parents. It was only two months later that my dad drew a line in the sand, saying he was tired of the drama, and couldn't handle the stress anymore. We haven't spoken since.

Honestly, I don't know when or if they will ever come around. Some days I'm more hopeful than others. Some days I have more grace for them than others. But what I do know is that in the process of refocusing my family, I found Clara. Other than the peace I've found in the center of God's grace, she's the best thing that's ever happened to me. She's become my family when my own family no longer had space. Committing my life to loving her was the best decision I've ever made.

17

SAYING "I DO"
TO A WOMAN

"Clara, I love you. Because of you, I laugh, I smile, I dare to dream again. You are my best friend and will be forever. Today, I give myself to you in marriage, to be your wife, secure in the knowledge that you will be my constant friend, my faithful partner, and my one true love. On this holy day, I give to you in the presence of God and these witnesses, my sacred promise, to love you without reservation, comfort you in times of distress, encourage you to achieve your goals, to laugh with you and cry with you, to cherish you and respect you, in sickness and in health, being open and honest with you always, for as long as we both shall live. I take you as my wife, and will give myself to no other. You have my whole heart for my whole life. And with everything I ever dreamed of standing right in front of me, I pledge my life to you."

The day I'd waited for all my life was finally upon me. I was about to marry the love of my life. In spite of my exhilaration, an unusual calm rested on me all day. But now, dressed in my long white wedding gown, I held tightly onto Mike Avila's arm.

My relationship with Mike and Loretta had only continued to deepen since meeting them at the Gay Christian Network conference in Phoenix a couple years prior. Now, as he prepared to walk me down the aisle and give me away to recite these vows, I began to shake; not because I was nervous—nothing in my life had ever felt more right—but because I was excited. I was about to walk down the aisle and pledge the rest of my life to

Mike Avila giving me away
on my wedding day

the woman I knew without a doubt God had created just for me. A contagious joy rose up inside me.

As Half Pint, our Flower Pup, walked down the aisle just before me, music from *Anne of Green Gables* played. It was my dream. As I walked down the aisle, "Somewhere in Time" played. That was Clara's dream. Looking at the faces of those present, I realized the crowd wasn't huge, but it was intentional. Each person was handpicked to be there due to their love and support of us. Each had responded to the invitation with "Yes" in affirmation of our love. And every guest who had come to share in our celebration was someone we knew on a personal level.

All of Clara's family was in attendance that day, sitting in the first two rows. Though they didn't necessarily understand or agree with our relationship, the importance of family in an Asian culture and their love for Clara won out over their need to be right. And on my side, a whole group of people from Highlands Church assumed the role of my honorary family and sat in the rows where my family would have been.

Looking back, I think we perplexed a lot of people at our ceremony. Yes, we were two women getting married, but our wedding was very intentionally Christ-centered and, in many ways, quite traditional. We had our ceremony in a church, we chose a former worship pastor from our church to marry us, we took communion, and we lit a unity candle. But knowing we were already unorthodox simply by being gay Christians, we added some creative elements to the mix.

One way we made it personal was by creating a short video that played just before the ceremony that told the story of how Clara and I had met. Following that, a conch shell blew just before Clara walked in, as a way to incorporate her Hawaiian

Taking communion together on our wedding day

upbringing. We wrote our own vows, and we asked both sets of parents (Clara's parents, as well as Mike and Loretta as my honorary ones) to pray a blessing over us and our marriage following communion. More than anything, we wanted it to be meaningful, Christ-centered, and memorable.

The day was everything I'd dreamed it to be. I wore the dress of my dreams, and it was white. I felt at peace, I felt content, I felt joy, and I felt so beautiful.

For many years I'd had a reoccurring dream. It was my wedding day, but as I walked down the aisle, something wasn't right. There was always an inherent feeling that the wedding was taking place out of pressure or obligation. Looking at the person I was about to marry (who was always a man) I thought, "I don't want to marry you. I don't love you." And then I'd wake up. For years, these dreams made me uneasy because I couldn't understand them. I never knew what those dreams meant until I realized I was gay. Then it made sense—I was supposed to marry a woman all along.

The missing piece to my heart was filled the day I married Clara. I gladly took her last name and made it my own. My life was on a fresh new path, and changing my name signified that.

The reception following the ceremony was filled with delicious food, laughter, dancing, and toasts from our very best

Praying a parental blessing over our union

friends. It was perfect. My best friend and Maid-of-Honor, Stacy, in her toast reminded everyone to never give up on their dreams.

"Leading up to Amber's wedding, I realized, you really can have the fairy tale. Your dreams really can come true. You can believe for anything!"

That's exactly how this felt to me. Dreaming as a young girl of my fairy tale wedding, my dreams were threatened for a time by a belief that love had limits. But once I was set free to love freely and openly, my fairy tale returned to me. Yes, I faced incredible loss in the process, but being who I was created to be, and finding the love of my life, brought me greater joy than I'd ever known.

• • • • •

In the Honeymoon Suite at a bed and breakfast that night with delivery pizza for our hungry stomachs, we opened each of the cards given to us by loved ones. Reading their thoughtful inscriptions brought us both joy and affirmation. It made us grateful for each of the amazing souls that God had placed in our lives. So many people had come alongside us in the months leading up to our wedding. Many of them were unexpected allies who gave of their time because of their love for the LGBT community and empathy for my lack of family support. A wedding planner with a gay brother volunteered her time to coordinate everything the day of the wedding so I didn't have to stress. A videographer with a gay sister gave us a significantly reduced rate so that we could have video footage of our special day. A lesbian caterer went above and beyond what we paid for to provide delicious food for our reception. Each one of these people were previously strangers, but in the planning process, became dear friends.

Then there were those who were more than friends—those who stood in as honorary family on my behalf. The part Mike and Loretta played in filling the role of my absent parents was exactly what I needed to get through the day. Loretta was there to help me get ready and put on my dress. Mike not only gave me away, but also prayed the parental blessing over us during the ceremony. He even agreed to the father-daughter dance.

In the weeks leading up to the wedding I had struggled a lot over whether or not I could even handle having a father-daughter dance. I knew it wouldn't be the *Butterfly Kisses* moment I'd always dreamed of having with my dad. But I also didn't want to regret not fulfilling that part of my perfect day just because my dad wasn't there to support me. So I asked Mike if he'd be willing.

"Whatever you need," he said. "We'll be there."

Mike and Loretta's presence, love, and support, along with those who stood in as my honorary family that day provided healing for me—like salve on a very tender and still-open wound.

In the bed and breakfast with my new wife that night, our hearts were full as we realized how blessed we were to have such amazing friends and family in our lives—some family by blood, some by choice—but all meaningful and valuable to us on the road we'd walked.

The final card we opened together was the one that had been kept in my hope chest since my thirteenth birthday. It was the one that, on the envelope read, "To My Future Husband." Just as intended, I brought it to open on our wedding night. Reading it together, we laughed at the childish fantasies, like having blue eyes and being a sports fan. We smiled at

My honorary family

my innocence. But more than anything else, we were grateful for the thread of loving Christ that had carried through to my adulthood. Looking back, it would have been so easy, with all my struggles, to walk away from my faith. It would have been so simple, with all the rejection I faced in the name of God, to turn my back on Christianity completely. But grace had kept me close to God's presence.

It's so obvious that God is in the midst of our marriage. There's such integrity, such love, such devotion in Clara. I am a better person, a stronger person, and a more complete person because I share my life with her. There's nothing more beautiful than that.

Though I had to do some refocusing in my views and beliefs to get to this place, I finally had a place to belong and someone to call my family forever. My heart was home at last.

18

REFOCUSING MY FAMILY

In early 2016, I sat across the dinner table from the national trans advocate and former megachurch pastor, Rev. Dr. Paula Williams. I told her I was thinking of going public with my story and asked if she had any advice for me. She sat calmly, probing a bit, and asked me a series of difficult questions. Feeling a little like I was being interrogated, it was clear to me she was getting at something; I just wasn't sure what it was. Then, after collecting the information she felt she needed, she looked me in the eyes with an intensity that came both from a heart of love and a heart of compassion, and said, "Amber, embedded in your identity is a *responsibility* to be a voice for change."

I sat with that profound statement and let it resonate for a moment. It felt like God in human form had just spoken to me. It was a divine moment that confirmed what I already felt I was supposed to do with the story I'd been given. Struck with both the weight of that responsibility and the magnitude of it, that phrase repeated itself in my spirit for days. That's how I knew it was God. And that's how I knew it was time to tell my story.

It's not an easy story to tell. Writing it has taken me on quite a journey. But I believe that part of the reason I'm still alive today is so that my story could be used to help change the culture for those still searching for hope to live authentically.

Lesbian, gay, and bisexual youth are four times more likely to attempt suicide than their straight peers, and LGB youth who come from highly rejecting families are over eight times more likely to attempt suicide compared to their LGB peers who report no or low levels of family rejection. 40 percent of transgender adults have reported attempting suicide with 92 percent of them doing so before the age of 25.

One of the driving forces behind writing this book was how close I came to being one of those statistics. The way family and friends respond to LGBTQ loved ones when they come out, directly affects their lives, and their perceived worth. I wish my parents understood that. It could have saved us all from so much heartache.

I'm so grateful for the life I have now and the joy I find in the family my wife and I are creating together. But looking back, I still think about my life in two parts: before coming out, and after coming out. In many ways, it feels like I've lived two completely different lives divided by one defining moment of authenticity. I've tried to blend those two worlds together whenever I can—like carrying on some of the traditions from my childhood. But when it comes to having my parents as a part of Clara's and my life, I've had to allow myself grace to accept the uncomfortable disconnect and grieve the loss.

In many ways, I'm still the same person I've always been. I still love music and have a strong passion for worship. I still love the holidays and fostering traditions that make them special. I still love creating a cozy home and hospitable environment. I still enjoy coaching and have a deep heart for people. And I still cuddle up next to the fireplace every fall for an *Anne of Green Gables* marathon. Being gay is just one part of who I am, but so much of me remains the same.

And at the same time, because I have been ostracized by people who want my sexuality to define me, much of me has changed. I've had to fight for my relationship with God against a culture that says you can't be both gay and Christian. I've had to study the Bible deeply for myself and learn how to defend my faith to those who question it. And I've had to look at issues through the eyes of the marginalized. I now stand with all people living in marginalized groups, whether I'm a part of them or not, because I believe that's what Jesus did, and because I've seen firsthand what happens to people when we don't. All of these things in turn have made me a stronger, healthier, and more well-rounded individual.

But in the process, I've also had to refocus a few things:

· · · · ·

First, I've had to refocus my worldview. I've stretched my understanding of God, become more tolerant of those I don't understand, and embraced diversity. What I've realized along my journey is that God comes in many forms. Far too often, we put God in a box, which as a result makes him substantially smaller than he really is. Since refocusing my worldview, I've seen God in different ethnicities, I've seen God in different religions, I've seen God in different sexual orientations and gender identities, I've seen God in the disabled and in those with special needs. If we look outside the rules of religion and expand our minds to a broader worldview, what we will see is that God is everywhere. We just have to open ourselves up to being more aware of the presence of God in our lives.

· · · · ·

I've also had to refocus my beliefs, especially those beliefs about the family unit. Being gay forced me to evaluate the belief I was taught by Focus and my parents—that there is only one type of family. In my case, that belief was challenged because I didn't have a choice. My sexuality put my life on the line and forced me to look this belief in the face. I realize that many other people have not yet confronted their beliefs when it comes to LGBTQ inclusion in the church because they haven't had to. There hasn't been anyone in their family or close circle of friends yet who has come out to them. But that doesn't mean they aren't there.

I am beyond grateful for those who, despite not having any direct link to the LGBTQ community, have taken the hard journey of challenging their old beliefs on this issue. It's not easy. It's a long, hard, painful, and often costly road to walk. But from the bottom of my heart, I thank you for your alliance and your love for us.

For those of you who have not yet walked the road, I implore you to start your own journey of refocusing. I know the fear you face is real. Coming from an upbringing where everything was cut and dried, black or white, right or wrong—there was no space for wondering. Knowing all the answers was critical to our faith. But what I've found is that questioning and uncertainty are not inherently bad. It doesn't mean your faith is weak. In fact, I think it takes even greater strength to ask the hard questions. But if you dig deep enough, I believe you'll discover a God bigger than your box.

It's only a matter of time before a family member or friend comes out to you. You need to be ready with an answer that reflects the true love of Jesus to them and nothing more. I can guarantee that whether you know who they are or not, there are LGBTQ people watching you, listening to what you say, and waiting to find that safe person in whom they can confide their deepest secret. I challenge you to be that person.

We have the opportunity to change the Focus on the Family legacy that says you can't be both gay and Christian. By doing the deep study and reflection of the Bible in its original language and thorough research of the culture and time in which the Bible was written, you will find that there is no place in the Bible that condemns homosexuality as we define it today. I am convinced that committed, monogamous, same-sex relationships and marriages are as blessed and sanctioned by God as those of committed, monogamous, straight relationships and marriages. By expanding the definition of the family unit to include those with same-sex parents, Christianity has the opportunity to embrace people who have been pushed to the fringes of society, largely by people acting in the name of God. Including LGBT people as equals in churches and Christian organizations will bring healing, renewal, and richness to the body of Christ.

There is room for all types of families within God's family—those with one male and one female parent, those with two male or two female parents, those with adopted kids, those with biological children, those with single moms or single dads, those with blended families, those with no kids—each one brings uniqueness, richness, and depth to the beautiful, diverse family of God. We need to shift our focus from black and white and refocus it to include the vibrant colors that those families who are currently living in the margins can offer.

· · · · ·

Finally, I've had to refocus my family. While the people in my family have changed, my values around family have remained very much the same. I just had to refocus my lens to see what's really important. Part of that was realizing my own worth in the family. I had to realize that my feelings, my need for acceptance, and my desire to belong were just as important as everyone else's, and that you don't always have to sacrifice your own happiness for the sake of others. Jesus told us to love your neighbor as you love yourself. But it's impossible to love your neighbor (who, by the way, is everyone) if you don't love yourself first. We must love ourselves as who God made us to be—image-bearers of Christ.

In the process of refocusing my family, I've learned that family isn't always blood. There's also chosen family—those you choose to do life with regardless of whether you have the same DNA. Some of the most incredible people I've ever met have only entered my life since coming out. Many have walked similar roads and struggled through similar journeys. Some are parents who have loved me like their own. But each of them holds a precious place in my heart and life.

I still cherish my family values, the commitment to family first, and the strengthening of the family bond just as much now as I did before coming out. In fact, I think it's become even more important to me because I've had to fight so hard for it. My wife, our two dogs, and the family we're creating together will always be the top priority in my life.

Refocusing my family has meant validating the value of the beautiful family I'm creating with my wife, as well as honoring the family values of my heritage. Doing that has been hard at times, but it's also made me stronger.

In all honesty, I still struggle. Some of my wounds have turned to scars, and some wounds still need to be healed. I still dream about my family. I still have PTSD and struggle with anxiety (though it has improved greatly with the help of my service dog and my wife). Holidays are still hard for me. And I still grieve for what could be.

At the time of the writing of this book, my parents have still not met Clara. They've never seen the beautiful home God has blessed us with, or the puppy we've added to our family. From the time Clara and I got married, my parents and I have had virtually no contact. They've missed so much of our lives, and I still wrestle through that pain daily.

I am a work in progress. I'm still healing from all the loss I've experienced. But I share my story with you because I believe more voices are needed to help change the narrative for LGBTQ Christians. As comfortable and easy as it is to live inside a box, sometimes our families, our beliefs, our worldviews need to be refocused. Sometimes what we've believed is wrong. Sometimes the way we understand our world is misinformed. Sometimes our families need balancing out.

Even though it's taken a lot of hard work to refocus my own perspectives in life, it's been worth it. It's led me into joy, it's led me into wholeness, and it's led me into being that voice for change that Paula Williams commissioned me to be. Yes, it's come at a cost, but the fullness that comes with authenticity has brought me so much freedom. In the end, authentic living has led me to the reward of having a stronger faith, and an even more focused family.

RECOMMENDED RESOURCES

Online Support Organizations:

Beyond (www.refocusingbeyond.org)

The Gay Christian Network (www.gaychristian.net)

The Reformation Project (www.reformationproject.org)

FreedHearts (www.freedhearts.org)

The Matthew Shepard Foundation (www.matthewshepard.org)

Inside Out Faith (www.insideoutfaith.org)

PFLAG (Parents, Family and Friends of Lesbians and Gays) (www.pflag.org)

It Gets Better Project (www.itgetsbetter.org)

Recommended Reading:

Changing Our Mind, by David Gushee

Does Jesus Really Love Me?, by Jeff Chu

God and the Gay Christian, by Matthew Vines

"Mom, I'm Gay", by Susan Cottrell

Risking Grace, by Dave Jackson

Torn, by Justin Lee

True Colors, by Susan Cottrell

Unclobber, by Colby Martin

Walking the Bridgeless Canyon, by Kathy Baldock

ACKNOWLEDGMENTS

To my wife, Clara—this book would not exist if it weren't for you. You encouraged me on my toughest days, you listened for hours as I dissected my life, you helped analyze and bring a fresh perspective, and more than anything, you believed in me. Thank you for all your support over the last many months. Life with you is an adventure worth living. I love you more than words can say. You have all of me.

To Fortress Press—thank you for investing in this story; for believing in it enough to help bring it to life. I am so grateful.

To my editors, Tony Jones and Lisa Gruenisen—thank you for your time and expertise in polishing my manuscript. You've helped make this book what it is.

To my beta readers—thank you for your patience as I fine-tuned this story and for your willingness to persevere through some really lousy drafts before getting to the good ones.

To my honorary family—you know who you are. Your love is like salve on a still-tender wound. Thank you for being there when I've needed you. A special thanks to:

Mike and Loretta Avila—thank you for assuming the huge role of parents on the day I needed parents the most. Thank you for loving me ever since.

Trish and Cliff Young—Thank you for instantly adopting both Clara and me as your granddaughters. You never hesitate to introduce us to others as family. That means so much to me. Nana, we have so much in common; you remind me of home. I love you.

Tracy Bray and Sue Moss—From the time I met you, you've felt like family. Thanks for being the ones I can call on in a pinch. You've been an integral part of my process and I'm so grateful for the loving and compassionate nature you both possess.

To Highlands Church—you've truly saved my life. Thank you for embracing me and showing me just how big the love of God really is. And thank you for continuing to be there and support me whenever I need you. It's an honor to call you family.

To the Mama Bears who have reached out to me—thank you for loving me like your own. I value your love more than you know.

To those who have followed, shared, written me, and been a part of this journey so far—this book is for you. You are the reason I write and the inspiration that gets me out of bed to work for equality each day.

And finally, I am thankful for the grace of God that carries me, the peace of God that surpasses my understanding, and the love of God that is indeed so much greater than I could have ever imagined.

"I pray that he may strengthen you with power through his Spirit in your inner being, so that Christ may dwell in your hearts through faith. And I pray that you, being rooted and established in love, may have power, together with all the Lord's holy people, to grasp how wide and long and high and deep is the love of Christ, and to know this love that surpasses knowledge—that you may be filled to the measure of all the fullness of God. Now to him who is able to do immeasurably more than all we ask or imagine, according to his power that is at work within us, to him be glory in the church and in Christ Jesus throughout all generations, forever and ever! Amen." —Ephesians 3:16–21 (NIV)

Me with James Dobson, Age 3

My first solo piano recital, Age 7

My first Anne of Green Gables birthday party

Putting on a home recital for family and friends

Performing my competition piece at an awards recital

Having an American Girl party with my GGG friends

*Signing my
Purity Pledge*

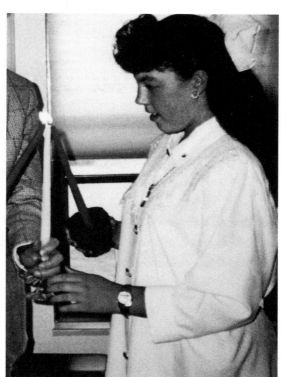

*Lighting a unity
candle with my Dad
to symbolize purity*

My Dearest Husband,

I am writing this letter to you, to let you know that I look forward to being your future wife. Even though I am just a young girl now, I truly want God's will in my life, and know He has chosen you for me. I want you to know that from now until I meet you, I will be comitted to pray for you, and for God's direction in your life. In Psalms 37:4, God tells us, "Delight thyself also in the Lord, and He shall give thee the desires of thine heart." These are the qualities I desire to have in a husband.

I desire that you:

Love the Lord with all of your heart
Trust in God, instead of in worldly things
Show respect to me
Are a good loving father and a wonderful husband
Are a faithful servant and work hard to accomplish everything
Have musical talents
Like children and enjoy playing with them
Have blue eyes
Enjoy playing sports
Are sharp and handsome (wearing no beard and maybe a mustache.)

I would also like you to know that from now, until our wedding day, I pledge to keep my body, my mind, and my heart totally pure, so that I can be the best wife for you that God intends me to be.

I love you, and look forward to sharing our lives together for the glory of God.

In His Hands,
Amber Nichole

The letter I wrote to my future husband at age 13

With Adventures in Odyssey actors: Walker Edmiston (Tom Riley, Left), Dave Madden (Bernard Walton, Back), Me (Front), and Katie Leigh (Condie Kendall, Right)

Doing an Adventures in Odyssey event for a Make a Wish Foundation child with Townsend Coleman (Jason Whittaker)

High school senior photo, age 16

Our wedding day

Our wedding day

Half Pint as the Flower Pup at our wedding

Our beautiful mix of blood and chosen family

Singing a song I wrote for Clara on our wedding day

Clara and me

Our family, aka The Cantorna Clan